This book is dedicated to my parents, Diane and Brian Hird, with my love.

Green IT in Practice

How one company is approaching the greening of its IT

GARY HIRD

IT Governance Publishing

IT Governance Publishing
IT Governance Limited
Unit 3, Clive Court
Bartholomew's Walk
Cambridgeshire Business Park
Ely
Cambridgeshire
CB7 4EH
United Kingdom

www.itgovernance.co.uk

First published in the United Kingdom in 2008 by IT Governance Publishing.

ISBN: 978-1-905356-61-4

This book has been produced on paper which is acid free and lignin free with no post-consumer waste. The cover paper is acid free with 20% post-consumer waste.

FOREWORD

There is a scientific consensus that we need to act rapidly to cut carbon dioxide emissions if we are to limit the most extreme effects of climate change. The IT sector is in a unique position to act as a catalyst for this change. By implementing simple efficiencies, the sector can reduce its carbon footprint – which currently is virtually the same size as that of the aviation industry. Crucially, the IT sector can play a major role in helping us all move to a low-carbon future by reducing the need for travel and enhancing communications.

Despite this potential for change, the IT sector has been surprisingly slow to address the issue of climate change. It is for this reason that the charity I founded, Global Action Plan, established the Environmental IT Leadership Team (EILT) – a unique advisory group consisting of major IT users seeking to make the use of IT more efficient. The first product of the EILT was a research report *An Inefficient Truth* which was launched at the end of 2007 at the House of Commons.

An Inefficient Truth illustrated the environmental impact of IT and the energy, security and supply issues associated with the huge growth within the sector. It explored the level of understanding that IT managers have around environmental issues and the challenges that they face internally, from vendors and from Government, in introducing more carbon-efficient policies. The report provided some practical examples demonstrating how a small number of organisations are starting to make a real difference in addressing this issue.

Gary Hird and The John Lewis Partnership have been important members of the Leadership Team and contributed to the production of the *Inefficient Truth* report and in the activities that the EILT is undertaking in 2008. If the IT sector is going to play the leading role it should in the fight against climate change then more practitioners like Gary are needed to enter into the debate, something that he is definitely doing with this book.

Trewin Restorick

Director

Global Action Plan

PREFACE

The objective of this book is to present some ideas for getting a 'Green IT' programme established or formalised within an organisation. It approaches this goal primarily by discussing the experience of one company, the John Lewis Partnership, in doing this during 2007 and the first half of 2008.

Chapters cover the link between general Corporate Social Responsibility and Green IT, how to go about constructing appropriate policies and metrics, and some thoughts on how to engage with employees and suppliers. Individual case studies on some key Green IT initiatives are then discussed in turn, before the book ends with a chapter considering how IT can begin to enable carbon footprint reduction in the organisation as a whole.

ABOUT THE AUTHOR

As Technical Strategy Manager for the John Lewis Partnership, Gary Hird is responsible for making sure that the company has the right strategy for its IT infrastructure and that this is fully aligned with business strategy.

Since 2006 Gary has taken responsibility for progressing Green IT initiatives for John Lewis and Waitrose.

ACKNOWLEDGEMENTS

The green mantra '*Reduce, Reuse and Recycle*' gives me an excuse for having drawn upon the work of many others in putting this book together. I'm confident I've done that with permission and appropriate acknowledgement in each case. Any glaring mistakes or omissions in the text are mine alone.

I'd like to thank all those at the John Lewis Partnership who have undertaken the Green IT projects at the John Lewis Partnership, or who have given their support and encouragement to that work or to the compilation of these pages. Particular thanks, in no particular order, go to Nick Monger-Godfrey, Gemma Lacey, Peter Jones, Gillie Cushine-Palmer, Norman Swift, Mark Turner, Joo McGread, Crispin Hobbs, Richard Willmott, Steve Parker, Bob Player, Gordon Siggers, Paul Woolfson, Tony Godwin, Ian Farr, Chris Eason, Charles Morris-Cox, Stephanie Coysten, Bill Wright, Paul Todd, Tony Austin, Martin Norris, John Keeling, Susan Donovan, Simon Tompsett, John Meredith, Dave Tarrant, Dominic Reddin, Ed Conway, Frank Cordrey, Gary Farr, Peter Dixon, Sam Hinton-Smith, Sarah Oliver and Simon Boase.

Dave Barker's help, in particular his continued indulgence of my penchant for colourful lifecycle diagrams and supporting spreadsheets, accepting that he then gets all the hard work behind them, has been very much appreciated.

Trewin Restorick and all at Global Action Plan deserve a big thank you for helping catalyse our work, for permission to quote from *An Inefficient Truth*, and for Trewin's foreword, as do all those involved with the EITL team, and Sarah Loftus from Anglian-Water-by-way-of-tif.

Many of our suppliers merit thanks too, and I'd give particular mention to Steve Bowden and Martin Lumsdon from IBM, Ted Shand and Jane Wass from BT, Lisa Fretwell from Cisco, Simon Mingay and Rakesh Kumar from Gartner, and Chris Gabriel from Logicalis.

I've benefited hugely from meeting with those responsible for Green IT at many different companies, notably at conferences such as the CIES summit on Green IT in April 2008. Conversations with Catriona MacAlistar representing DEFRA, and with Steve O'Donnell (ex-BT) were particularly helpful.

I owe a particular debt to Catalina McGregor from the Ministry of Defence, who is taking the lead for the United Kingdom on two of four major working groups for Green IT in Brussels, and with the OECD. She and Chris Head from SOCITM were kind enough to share with me the material that forms the basis of the checklist appendix.

I owe David Richards a thank you again for his blessing for the John Lewis Partnership to adapt Yell group's original funnel diagram. Our variant is reproduced in Chapter 3.

I'm sure I have inadvertently missed a number of people who deserved mention, and for that I apologise.

CONTENTS

INTRODUCTION

There's a bewildering mass of information to sift through for managers involved with a programme of Green IT work.

This guide is intended to help you navigate through all that information a little more easily by giving it a structure and by outlining some practical examples of techniques and solutions that IT departments, including my own, have adopted in this area.

It is not meant to be a detailed technical guide, a long list of statistics, a prescriptive 'do this or the earth gets it' set of laws, or a boast that I know all the answers. (I certainly don't!) It's partly for those scared by terms such as 'ISO14001 compliance' and who are looking for an alternative way to get started.

So hopefully you will find it helpful. And if not, well, I'm acutely aware that, even if you purchased this in eBook format, this book has a carbon footprint of its own (I haven't attempted to calculate precisely what that is, I'm afraid). So, if having read the suggestions in the following chapters, you feel that the book simply wasn't worth the carbon needed to produce it, I'm sure some appropriate way to reuse or recycle the pages will suggest itself to you!

Whatever its merits now, I'd like to think that this book will have become redundant in a few years' time: the ideas referenced here will by then have become an 'unconscious competency' (to use one of the labels from Chapter 3) being practised effectively by the majority of IT departments; and of course a whole new raft of innovative ideas for using IT to further reduce companies' carbon footprints will have emerged.

We'll see. Meanwhile, I'd like to wish you good luck in all that you do to improve the environmental credentials of your organisation's IT. I'm also happy to hear from you about your own experiences in progressing a green agenda. You can contact me at gary_hird@johnlewis.co.uk.

CHAPTER 1: WHAT IS GREEN IT?

'Green computing', like anything with a 'green' tag, can be hard to define. The label means different things to different people, and an IT department getting to grips with the subject can find it useful to start by trying to determine exactly what it understands by the term.

I've used the following definition to describe a green programme of IT work:

Green IT is a collection of strategic and tactical initiatives which either:

- directly reduce the 'carbon footprint' of the organisation's computing operation;
- use the services of IT to help reduce the organisation's overall carbon footprint;
- incentivise and support greener behaviour by the organisation's employees, customers and suppliers;
- ensure the sustainability of the resources used by IT.

The first of the categories above is where most of the focus of Green IT (including the case studies and examples in this book) has been over the past couple of years. However, a green computing action plan should also look beyond what the IT organisation is doing internally, and explore the possibilities for IT to act as an enabler for greening the rest of the company (potentially this is the area with the opportunity to make the biggest positive impact on a company's carbon footprint). An example might be the development of a computer system to allow more intelligent vehicle scheduling for the organisation's supply chain fleet.

The questions IT departments need to ask themselves right at the start, before launching into the 'how we get there' detail, are

- Why are we doing this?
- How green are we currently?
- How green do we want to be (and how soon)?

These questions will have different answers for different organisations working in different industry sectors. It is important that the IT department doesn't simply try to answer the questions in isolation based on its own position, without placing them in the context of the overall green agenda of the organisation.

For some companies, the answer to *Why are we doing this?* is simply a need to reduce overall energy costs. Other motivations may include a desire to improve customer confidence in the company's products or services. It may be a matter of satisfying shareholders, meeting regulatory obligations or avoiding costs because of the environmental impact of the company's actions. Some may be mindful of media attention or keen to foster a reputation as a green organisation for competitive advantage. Employees' concerns or even prospective employees' expectations may influence some firms, while some will be looking to generate income by selling excess emissions allowances. And a few companies will still have a 'why indeed?' stance and be unconvinced by any of the above reasons of the need to act. Thankfully, this last group is becoming a smaller and smaller minority.

Essentially, all of the reasons *why?* boil down to one of three overlapping drivers – reputation, cost, or company culture.

Often the IT department's green aspirations will simply reflect the organisation's overall green aspirations, which are in turn a reflection of its 'corporate culture'. If there is a significant difference between the two, so that the green aspirations of an IT department significantly lead or lag the organisation's overall green agenda or current credentials, then it's worth knowing that as soon as possible, and the implications and perceptions of such a difference should be considered.

Too big a lag, and the advice to the IT department might be to start doing something soon before it is imposed from outside. A big lead and there is both an opportunity for IT to take a thought-leadership role in shaping the company's overall green agenda but also a potential threat to the funding of any Green IT initiatives if the organisation has not bought in to the merits of such a programme.

When considering the next question, *How green are we currently?*, my advice would be to address it simply. A good old-fashioned workshop session is probably the best way to gather the information you need. This is how we kicked off the Green IT programme within the John Lewis Partnership's IT department. I recently dusted off the flipchart output from the first workshop on this subject, which I conducted towards the end of 2006 with colleagues from a cross-section of IT teams. On that occasion we simply used coloured cards to compile a list of 'statements' reflecting our existing green capabilities and significant gaps in capability.

Here are a few verbatim examples from that exercise:

- We measure datacentre electricity usage, but have less of an idea how much non-datacentre IT electricity we use. Ideally we'd like to measure usage in a more 'granular' way.
- We are supplied with manufacturers' ratings for their equipment but these are not always easy to find and we have no easy way to compare these fairly and consistently.
- We don't measure the power we need for cooling.
- As a result of the recent VMware consultancy, we know that our utilisation rate for Wintel servers is approximately 8 per cent.
- We are fully WEEE[1] compliant for IT, and we can measure/test this through site visits to the supplier. The cost of this arrangement is likely to increase this year.
- We perceive other recycling (e.g. paper, or packaging) in the department as an area we could improve.
- Because our systems are designed for resilience, half of the asset (or footprint) at any one time is not doing anything.
- We have some very old servers which cost us money to maintain.
- We make limited use of videoconferencing.
- We perceive our travel costs as too high.
- We comply with ROHSS rules for new servers.

---

[1] European Community directive 2002/96/EC on waste electrical and electronic equipment (WEEE)

Having considered the first two questions, *Why are we doing this?* and *Where are we currently?*, it's time to move on and answer the third.

The next chapter suggests some useful ways to proceed.

CHAPTER 2: HELP TO GET STARTED

Visit your CSR department!

I can't recommend highly enough the benefits of engaging early with those in your organisation responsible for Corporate Social Responsibility (CSR). Yet many of the IT staff from other companies I have spoken to over the past couple of years do not seem to have done this to any significant degree when getting to grips with the topic.

In the John Lewis Partnership (JLP) I have been very lucky right from the very beginning of the green programme of work. We have an excellent CSR capability and our then Head of Corporate Social responsibility, Nick Monger-Godfrey, and his colleague Gemma Lacey, were only too happy to meet with me as needed and to provide guidance on how to tackle the problem. Much of this next section borrows directly from their work describing the way in which CSR in general is addressed at JLP. I soon found that just about all of this can be applied to the processes needed to establish and mature a Green IT programme.

The process for managing CSR in JLP involves six main steps:

1 Identify and map out the important CSR issues.
2 Gather views from internal and external stakeholders on the importance of these issues.
3 Risk-assess the issues based on legal compliance, cost and business opportunity.
4 Prioritising which issues to lead and 'champion' based on the previous step.
5 Continuously measure our performance.

6 Set improvement targets and objectives.

The following few paragraphs discuss in turn these general CSR processes, as described by Nick and Gemma, and then I indicate in **bold** how that has been applied (if indeed it has) to our Green IT programme.

A large number of issues are grouped under the CSR heading. To map them out we group them into issues affecting four main areas:

- the natural environment
- local people and communities
- our customers and suppliers
- our employees ('Partners').

For IT, we definitely needed some sort of taxonomy. I considered various groupings but in the end found it most useful to group initiatives based on the four lifecycle areas of 'design', 'procurement', 'use' and 'disposal'.

There are many different stakeholder groups who care about these issues and we have to consult each carefully to understand their views. It is not unusual for different stakeholder groups to prioritise these issues differently. For example, our partners may care about work–life balance, Greenpeace about the sustainability of our timber, Government about climate change, and customers about over-packaging. **It is important to have clearly addressed stakeholder views on Green IT from both within the IT department and from outside. I have included some specific ideas and examples on how to do this in the 'challenges to employees and suppliers' chapters later in this book.**

We prioritise the various CSR issues based on risk and opportunity. We look at current legislation, business cost, reputational risk (based on stakeholder opinion surveys), business opportunity (the importance to our customers) and how easy/difficult it is for us to change. This enables us to draw up a list of key issues to focus on. That doesn't mean that we exclude others; we just clearly define those which we wish to lead on. **For IT, the prioritisation exercise early in 2007 was very rudimentary – it was a case of identifying that our first two 'horses to back', those where most of the efforts of those involved would be concentrated, would be server virtualisation and desktop power management (using 'wake-on-LAN' software). Since then, we've put in place a slicker process for evaluating and prioritising Green IT initiatives, and I discuss this in the next chapter.**

When we have identified those important issues, we have to decide for each how far to go – *How green is good enough?* We consider three elements (*see Figure 1*):

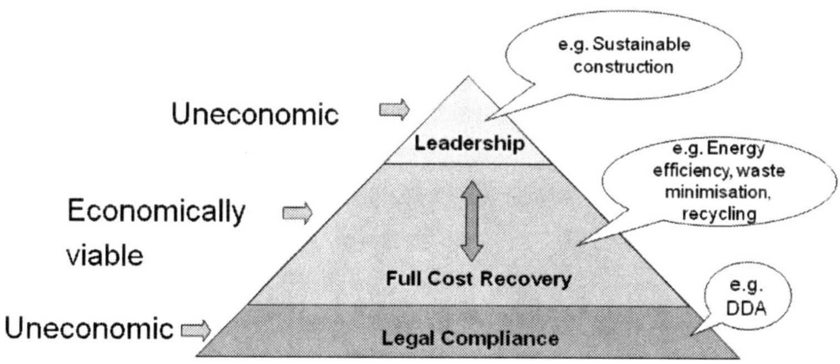

Figure 1: Defining success

a) Compliance

Regardless of cost, we must clearly ensure that we meet our legal requirements (such as, for example, the requirements of new laws on disability and access and building design). Inevitably there is a cost of compliance or, in many cases, there is no economic return on any investment we make to ensure legal compliance. **Within IT we have to make sure we comply with the specific, relevant regulations, such as WEEE, the Waste Electrical and Electronic Equipment Directive.**

b) Full cost recovery

It is in our commercial interest to use less energy, drive fewer miles, generate less waste and recycle more, and we must reduce our impacts in these areas to the absolute minimum where the investment and payback is acceptable. **Most of the Green IT initiatives we have pursued at JLP have fallen into this category**.

c) Leadership

This is where we may choose to 'set an example' and adopt a position of leadership on some issues which may not make economic sense, but are core to our values or customer proposition. **The assessment of which Green IT initiatives make economic sense is not a one-off exercise, as the economics of solutions changes with time. ('Should TCO be replaced by what we might instead call T-CO2?' one delegate joked at a recent conference.) The view of what a true *leadership* initiative is will also change over time, of course. Today's initiatives that fit into that category will almost certainly come to be regarded in time as tomorrow's 'table stakes'.**

(A short aside – one possible approach for justifying leadership elements of a Green IT programme, which would otherwise be dismissed as uneconomic, is to directly channel the additional costs saved by implementation of full cost recovery solutions into funding those leadership projects. This would mean that, although they would otherwise not have a compelling individual cost case, the work can proceed as long as the overall basket of green initiatives is cost neutral. We regard this as an interesting approach to funding Green IT initiatives, but it is not one that we have decided to implement at JLP.)

Following the prioritisation of issues, it is important that we set out our future expectations and targets. To be transparent we must also share these ambitions publicly. It is easy to look back and show we have made progress, but much harder to set challenging targets and then work to achieve them. **We maintain a monthly 'steering wheel' of key performance indicators (KPIs) within the IT department, using a traffic light scheme (where red is below target, amber is a near miss, green is on or above target) to show at a glance the operational performance of our IT, key project milestones, financial control of budgets and so on. We are not yet routinely reporting on the many possible Green IT KPIs or subsidiary performance indicators, so Green IT reporting has been a separate per-project exercise until now, but we are starting to identify the measures we need to add into this monthly KPI summary.**

We have set public CSR targets for both John Lewis and Waitrose since 2004 and we publicly report our performance each year in our CSR report and on our website. **We are not yet at the stage where we are doing this against targets for the *greenness* of our IT, but we**

are now at least starting to publicise within the company the initiatives we have underway and where we are with these, using the 'acorns' diagram which I discuss in the next chapter.

Some longer-term targets

As a taste of things to come, here are some targets we might choose to set ourselves based on the excellent work of the UK Government's DEFRA Market Transformation Programme for energy consumption of computing equipment:

- 2013: average sleep mode for desktops – less than 3 watts (W);
- 2014: average off/standby for laptops – less than 1W;
- 2020: average on-idle consumption for desktops – less than 45W;
- 2020: average on-idle consumption for laptops – less than 9W;
- 2020: average on-active consumption for monitors – less than 25W.

(The Market Transformation Programme supports UK Government policy on sustainable products, collecting data to quantify the current and future environmental impact. It then works with stakeholders to ensure development of products that will have a lower impact on the environment throughout their life cycle by using less energy, water and materials and producing less waste. Further details are at www.mtprog.com.)

Other sources of help

There is a variety of green conferences at which you can learn more about the specifics of particular technologies, and other groups have formed to offer help to organisations' Green IT efforts, whether in a particular industry sector or more generally. It's worth remembering that your time is finite, though – and you'll need most of it to actually implement some of what you've learned.

I make no apology here for publicising the work of a group that JLP has been a member of for the past year, one that I have found particularly helpful. The Environmental IT Leadership Team (EILT) was set up by the Global Action Plan charity, which has a long track record of successfully helping organisations to reduce their environmental impact.[2]

I'll be quoting examples elsewhere in this book from the research report *An Inefficient Truth,* the title a deliberate nod to Al Gore's similarly titled film on climate change. The report was launched at the end of 2007 by the EILT.

The Corporate IT Forum ('tif.') can also be a very useful way for member organisations to share experiences or benchmark progress, and tif. have facilitated a number of events themed around Green IT topics.[3]

It is great when such groups start to use the collective power of their members to deal with the thornier issues facing us all (such as influencing a particular manufacturer's licensing policy). In a similar vein, I'd also encourage you to be as open as you possibly can be with

---

[2] www.globalactionplan.org.uk
[3] www.tif.co.uk

your competitors about Green IT initiatives. For most industries this is not an area to protect for competitive advantage.

Find out what's already happening

I've talked about 'starting' a Green IT programme as though a mere vacuum existed beforehand, but of course this is never the case, and you may find that there are many relevant but isolated pieces of work which have either already happened, are underway or have been identified as candidate projects. You will certainly find allies early on in your IT teams who have been quietly investigating what is possible in their own specialist areas. They will be only too happy to share details with you if you ask.

Ask suppliers for help

There is a chapter later about engaging with suppliers so I won't say much on the subject here, other than to recommend that you actively solicit help from all of your key suppliers to support your green initiatives and also ask them what initiatives they recommend you should be considering. It is fashionable to dismiss the motives of IT suppliers as 'greenwash' and you will certainly encounter this in some quarters, but you will also come across some very genuine and committed experts.

The bibliography at the end of this book gives more suggestions on where to look for help.

CHAPTER 3: WHAT TO DO AND HOW TO MEASURE IT

Policies

As companies start to formulate Green IT policies, some of these are being driven from a top-down approach and some are bottom-up. Most involve a combination of the two.

A top-down Green IT policy might be a bold statement, something like: *Our organisation's IT will be carbon-neutral by 2011*. It might be directly related to a company's mission statement to reduce its footprint by a certain percentage by 2020 compared to a 2000 figure, say. The difficulty is in translating that high-level objective into the concrete effort that will actually deliver it.

The alternative approach of pulling together a policy in a bottom-up approach means identifying, classifying and bunching together various individual policies, such as: *We will virtualise every new server unless there is a documented and agreed reason not to*.

However, the situation in many companies following the bottom-up approach can be summed up as: *In our company we have lots of individual policies that deliver Green IT, but no overall Green IT policy.*

One company I spoke to recently had so many individual policies that they felt this had started to prove counter-productive, and they were now instead concentrating on management of behaviour.

It appears that many companies are attempting both top-down and bottom-up approaches simultaneously, which I think is a practical necessity for many, but which I'd also liken to digging the Channel Tunnel from both ends. It is fine if France and Britain meet up in the middle but a nightmare they don't!

It also presents an accountability issue – if your organisation issues a top-down decree that says, for example: *We must cut our carbon footprint by 10 per cent by 2015*, and all departments including IT are expected to achieve that, then IT needs to demonstrate that its bottom-up work is truly helping meet the top-down initiative (or it needs to be able to demonstrate that its carbon footprint is outweighed by the carbon savings in the rest of the business that IT systems enable). To do that effectively we need a baseline to refer back to.

A policy is no good without an understanding of why that policy exists, who owns the policy, a good mechanism for monitoring and policing compliance is in place, together with mechanisms to measure the actual effectiveness of that policy and review its relevance and continued suitability.

Metrics

Before making any change to improve your green credentials, it is helpful to understand where you are now and to have effectively baselined the IT department's current carbon footprint (or at least the components of that). Without that baseline it can be difficult to demonstrate the impact Green IT initiatives will have in practice.

Deciding what to measure can be a tricky business, as can working out how to measure it fairly and in a way that is readily repeatable. There is also the question of how to interpret what you're measuring. Once you've seen an improvement in a particular metric, how can you be sure you know exactly which of the many initiatives you undertook in that area actually achieved your saving?

IT departments also need a way to assess 'best practice' and how their performance matches up against that, before prioritising the initiatives which will help plug that gap. On top of all that, best practice itself doesn't stand still, so you need to track what new initiatives others are pursuing to further improve IT's green credentials.

Here are just a few examples of practical Green IT metrics it is possible to use:

- percentage utilisation of the Intel estate of servers (or similar for Unix) – should be as high as is practical;
- print cartridges consumed per year;
- paper consumed per user per year (perhaps broken down by site giving an opportunity to engineer a competition between areas as to which users are greenest);
- PUE – 'power utilisation equation' value for the datacentre;
- percentage of desktops being automatically switched off overnight;
- number of cathode ray tube (CRT) screens still in operation within the company;
- temperature to which the datacentre is cooled.

Arguably, there should also be a metric on the effort and time needed to collect the IT department's green metrics and report on these each time. Improving and automating this 'collection effort' will mean that you will not repeatedly need considerable expense and/or effort just to reassess the progress you have made since last measuring.

These are all bottom-up metrics associated with bottom-up policies. Companies may instead start to require IT to provide figures expressed in tonnes of CO_2 for its current and forecast carbon footprint, and to be able to break that overall figure down into its constituent elements. But the act of carbon calculating can sometimes feel a bit like constructing an astrology chart, and I've therefore wondered whether, if we were to ever conduct two different independent assessments of the same IT carbon footprint, it would be like reading two different newspapers' horoscopes for the same day. So, as we are likely to need to perform these assessments more systematically, they'll need to be based on calculations from a trusted authority, and we'll need to record which authority, and of course the assumptions made for a calculation; when it is repeated a year later, say, we can confidently measure true progress.

Sometimes, even though a project has had a significant positive environmental impact, it will have been overtaken by events and so the overall change in a metric from the baseline can be depressingly low. That is until those involved factor in, say, the infrastructure capacity growth over that same period, and show how bad the metric would have been without the action taken. This may influence the choice of what metrics to use – but ultimately what matters is the impact on the planet, so metrics that properly reflect that (rather than emphasising the positive change of a project and ignoring the negative effects outweighing it) are obviously the fairest to use.

We ought to also consider the metrics we may be expected to report on in a few years' time – what things should we be starting to measure regularly now so that we can provide an effective baseline for the future?

Gartner[4] have developed a comprehensive Green IT benchmarking initiative which some companies are now starting to use to more formally assess their green credentials against a common standard.

Initiatives

It's not just the world's natural resources that are limited. Your time is finite too. So given that your IT teams have a constrained amount of 'official' project hours available to spend, you need a way to select the initiatives which will bring you the best 'green return'.

A couple of years ago, I was asked to set up a day for a senior audience focusing on new technologies and how our company might exploit them. Although the attendees were by no means Luddites when it came to recognising the opportunities technology might enable, it was obvious there would still be a challenge in distilling 'techie-talk' into the information they would actually be interested in, which was:

- which initiatives we had underway;
- the possible business benefit of each (expressed as increased sales, reduced costs, increased business 'agility' and so on);
- the current status of each initiative;
- the likely time to fruition.

---

[4] www.gartner.com

On this occasion I constructed a 'funnel' diagram based on one that yell.com use, had demonstrated to us and have given me their blessing to adapt. The basic funnel template, prior to the technologies being inserted, is shown in Figure 2 with a single example.

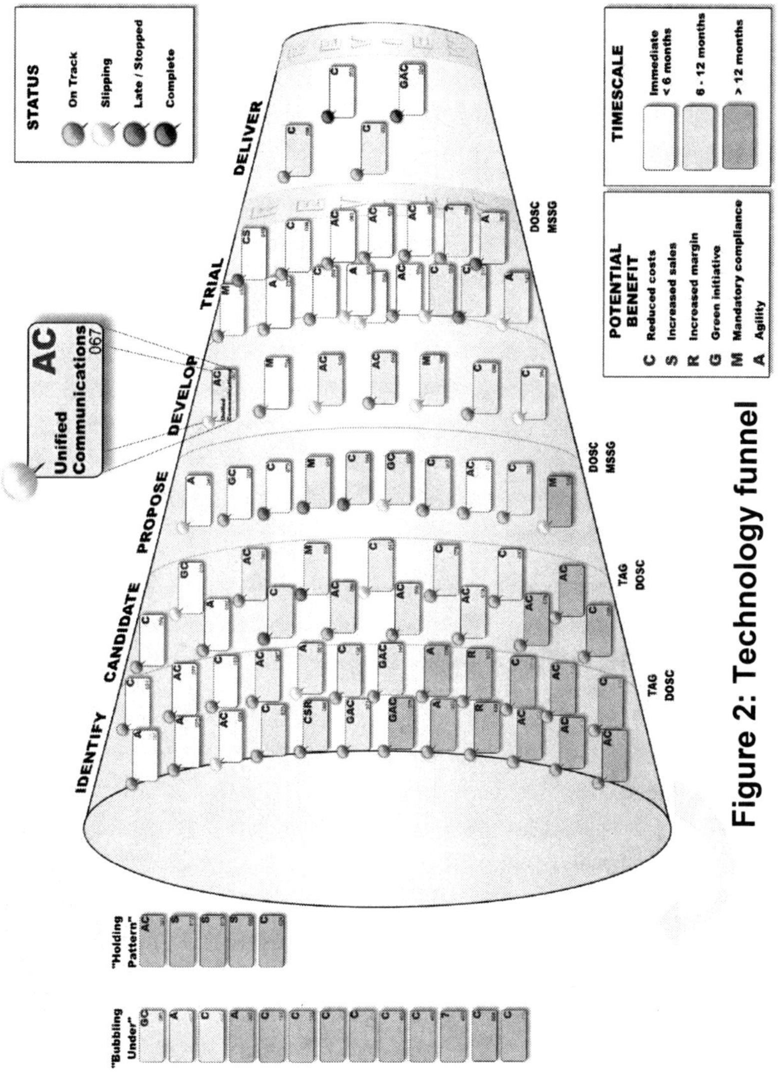

Figure 2: Technology funnel

It is a colourful and useful way of showing at a glance our progress in assessing, trialling and implementing the new technologies relevant to our business. Technologies progress from left to right on the funnel, which deliberately narrows in that direction because not every technology we assess will (or should) make it through the various stages of the process.

The diagram is now intended to be a 'living document', reviewed and updated every quarter by our technical architects, and issued to a subscription list of teams within the IT department, interested users (some of whom prefer a short set of presentation slides or an A3 landscape diagram to a discussion paper), and of course suppliers (we share a slightly sanitised version of the diagram with the outside world, with a couple of confidential projects removed, and don't share the spreadsheet behind the diagram which gives a little more company-sensitive information).

The attributes of each technology's entry on the diagram indicate its impact, potential business benefits and current project status. The phases or stages shown on the funnel are:

- **Identify:** this column on the diagram shows new technologies that have been identified (by an individual or team) as potentially being of widespread benefit.
- **Candidate:** a technology is in this column if the technical architects have collectively agreed that it is of potential benefit to our business. Usually at this stage we are considering suppliers' offerings in this technology area.
- **Propose:** this stage is reached when a formal proposal has been written recommending the use of the technology and providing a cost–benefit case for it.

- **Develop:** this is once a project has been agreed, and work is being performed to build solutions, define business processes and ensure that a suitable solution is in place via testing, ready for the trial/pilot.
- **Trial:** a limited trial of the technology is underway.
- **Deliver:** the technology is being used in a live environment, although not necessarily company-wide.

There are two further columns on the left-hand side of the diagram, outside the funnel. The far left one contains initiatives which are currently **'bubbling under'** the funnel with only practical constraints (such as someone suitable having time to progress them) keeping them from being progressed.

The other column reflects the fact that when we reject technologies we are sometimes simply saying that it is not right for our company now rather than not right for us at all, so effectively it consists of initiatives which have previously been in the funnel and are now in a **'holding pattern**' waiting for the time to be right for them to be reassessed.

The focus of the funnel is on technologies that are within 12–18 months of delivery. We also maintain (twice a year) a radar diagram (*see the template in Figure 3*) and supporting material of technologies that are more 'blue-sky' in nature, anything up to 10 years or so away from delivery. The size of each blip on the radar indicates the likely impact of the corresponding technology. When a blip gets within a year of the centre of the radar we would expect it to turn into an item on the funnel.

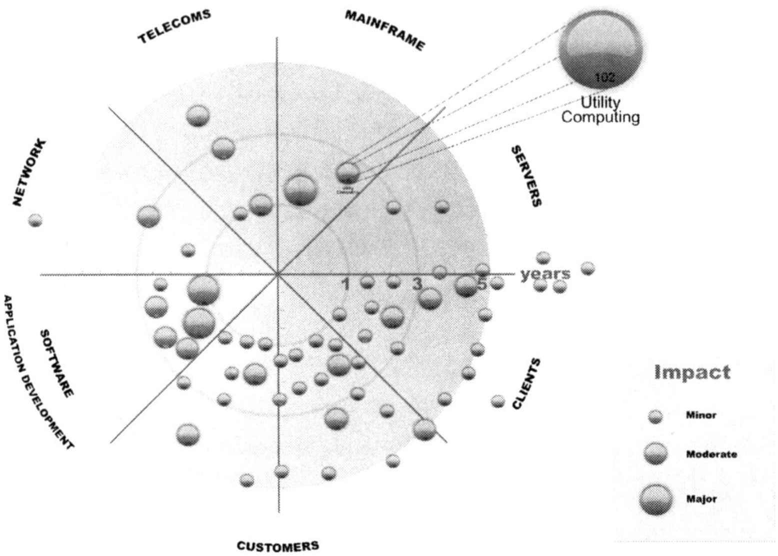

Figure 3: Technology radar

To complete the set of diagrams, we're interested in making sure that our portfolio of infrastructure technologies, software languages and tools is not larger than it should be. So technologies that are due to be retired in the next three years appear in our 'graveyard' (*see the template in Figure 4*). Each gravestone on the diagram shows who is responsible for killing the technology off, the effort of killing it, the impact of not killing it, when it should die and what will replace it.

Figure 4: Technology graveyard

The acorns diagram

These diagrams have proved successful as a way of communicating progress to the department, so when our work on Green IT really got going it was natural to think about how we might do something similar for the various initiatives underway via a similar diagram. Initially, we bolted a green element onto the funnel diagram itself as another potential business benefit attribute of the technologies we were assessing. It became clear, however, given that green initiatives are so diverse, cover so many areas of the IT department and are described in different ways to the funnel new technologies, that a separate spreadsheet and diagram would be required.

We're just starting to use this tool, which for want of a better name we have called the 'Green IT acorns' diagram (*see the template in Figure 5*).

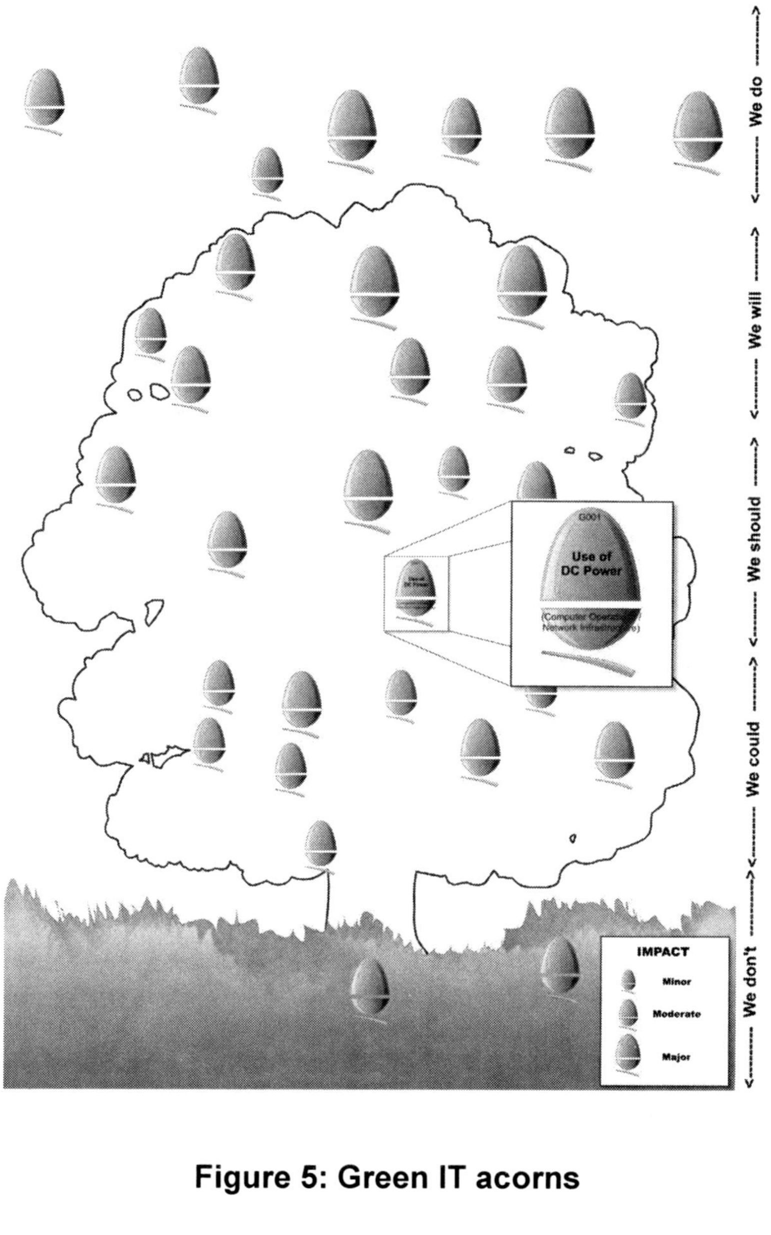

Figure 5: Green IT acorns

Pictures are all very well and a good way to communicate at-a-glance, but these technology lifecycle diagrams only really come into their own when used with the information behind them. Behind the acorns diagram is a spreadsheet, with one row for every Green IT initiative we've taken forward in the company over the past two years. The spreadsheet columns contain the attributes for each initiative, the first few of which are:

- a description of what the piece of work is, together with a short rationale for proceeding with it;
- space for consideration of why we might not want to do this (other than for reasons of cost or effort);
- a short description of what needs to happen in practice to effect this change;
- whether the effort in time to implement is low, medium or high;
- whether the cost to implement is low, medium or high;
- the likely impact or benefit (low, medium, high plus details);
- whether this benefit is likely to be measurable – financially or quantifiably – and how we will measure progress;
- for those actions already underway, a 'current status and next steps' column, to allow us to track progress.

So far so good, but nothing particularly distinguishes this from any candidate project list. We also attempt to categorise the actions in a few additional ways:

1 Lifecycle stage

- Is this a **Design** issue of some sort?

- Does it relate to **Procurement** of software, hardware or services?
- Is it an issue relating to our **Use** of IT equipment?
- Is it a **Disposal** issue?

We allow for a category of **Other** just in case real life doesn't quite fit into our lifecycle silos.

The original categorisation we used here, courtesy of tif., was equally valid, but a different way of cutting the problem, and was as follows:

- Is the initiative related to **Communication** within the company?
- Does the initiative relate to our **Equipment** e.g. server or printer estate?
- Does it concern purchase of **Consumables** (IT supplies)?
- Is this a **Supplier** issue?
- Is it a **Travel** issue?
- Does it relate to our **Property** e.g. energy efficiency of our buildings?]

2 Involvement/responsibility of the IT department.

- Is the initiative an IT action which is therefore entirely for us to **Own**? In which case, which team or area is driving progress?
- Or is it a business action already identified which IT can **Enable**?
- Or is it an action for IT to **Propose** (we think the merits of doing it should be considered or we think it should be done)? In which case, by whom, how will the decision be taken, and how?

3 Current competency

This is a measure of how ingrained a green behaviour is within the department or the company. The analogy I like to use is of a new driver, who might start out aged 17 as a learner, unaware that they don't really know how to drive properly, through the dawning realisation that the Highway Code and 'mirror-signal-manoeuvre' needs to be learned properly, through the gradual steady improvement in ability that practice and mentoring brings, through to a stage where good driving is second-nature. In other words, the driver follows a path from unconscious incompetence to conscious incompetence to conscious competence to unconscious competence.

So the question we ask ourselves here for each green initiative or behaviour is as follows:

- Within the IT department or the company generally, are we currently unconsciously incompetent (UI) on this issue – there's possibly a need for us increase our understanding of what the issue actually is, or to raise awareness elsewhere?
- Or are we consciously incompetent (CI) – we know there's something we could be better at but we're not doing it (maybe there's a practical obstacle to overcome first before we can)?
- Or are we consciously competent (CC) – the green behaviour is one that we're doing or starting to do but it hasn't yet become business-as-usual?
- Or have we reached the unconsciously competent (UC) stage – the green behaviour has become second-nature to us, ingrained in our ways of working?

In practice we decided that we needed labels for these four stages that are less of a mouthful, and that don't run the risk of us causing offence to anyone who might take exception to a label of 'incompetent' (we considered 'incapable' only a slightly less-risky alternative). So on the acorns diagram we use a pseudo-scale running from the discarded acorns (not every green initiative is right for our infrastructure) at the bottom of the tree, with the labels 'We don't', 'We could', 'We should', 'We will' and 'We do' at the top of the tree.

4 Compliance vs. full cost recovery vs. leadership (as per the previous chapter)

The spreadsheet also has a column which we can use to flag the initiatives we feel should have the highest priority, given the previous analysis. We group related initiatives together; for example, we might have ten or so individual datacentre environmental initiatives underway, but we group these rows together in the spreadsheet.

The acorns diagram is undeniably a gimmick, but then it is partly designed to be – we wanted something that catches the eye and engages people. An equally valid, slightly more sober way of representing progress against Green IT issues might be a tif. bull's-eye diagram using categories such as 'travel', 'consumables' etc. as sectors and placing initiatives nearer to the centre based on the competency assessment earlier.

Work planning

What I've described above is an extra process set up specifically for Green IT, which is designed to help communicate progress within the IT department and to interested others. It is at least as important to embed some green thinking into the standard work-planning process.

We've started with something simple here, a flag on our candidate projects work-plan list to try and determine if there would be any green impact (whether positive or negative) linked to a particular candidate, with another column for details if we had them.

We are confident that as we prepare for the next round of work planning we will start to see that greenness flag helping us make prioritisation decisions which more formally take account of *green* as a driver. However, ultimately we believe work planning and cost cases for individual proposals will need to include a more sophisticated carbon impact assessment.

How you choose to govern the processes for setting policies, metrics (including targets) and initiatives will differ from company to company. At JLP we found it simplest to have the green work feeding into existing governance groups.

CHAPTER 4: DESIGN TO DISPOSAL – SOME ISSUES TO CONSIDER

This chapter examines each stage of the design–procure–use–dispose lifecycle in turn and gives for each one a few brief examples of Green IT issues and considerations. I've concentrated for this chapter on elements of Green IT not covered elsewhere in the book. For example, virtualisation technologies aren't covered here under 'use' because they merit a whole chapter later in the book.

Design – 'coding green'

Programmers who have been around since the early days of corporate IT are sometimes heard to lament that we've lost the discipline of efficient coding. It was necessary back then to inventively squeeze as much processing into as few program instructions and as little storage space as possible. Nowadays, the implication is, freedom from such constraints has made us less good at programming.

However tempting it might be to regard this as nostalgia and nothing more, there is a serious message. Software 'bloat', especially in the packages we buy, is a green issue and not merely a rose-tinted one. Optimally tuning application performance should be on our green agendas, too. And if reuse is the first of the '3 Rs of green' (Reduce, Reuse, Recycle), then surely software reuse also needs to figure in our green thinking somehow.

There are other green design issues too. Given how much of the carbon footprint of a server, laptop or desktop is in its manufacture, it clearly isn't right for us to need to replace perfectly good hardware until we really need to. (There is a whole separate discussion to be had elsewhere about when is the optimum time to replace IT equipment.) But yet, that is essentially what some software packages have made necessary, ever since the rise of the PC.

Many architecture decisions (for example which hardware platform to host applications on, whether to code for a thin or thick client) have energy implications. An example of the type of question IT departments need to start asking themselves is this:

If it emerges that one platform has significantly greener credentials than another (and the latest mainframe models are making a good case currently, given their 100% utilisation capability and the energy costs for the processing they do) then to what degree will/should this shape our hardware platform roadmaps and the priority which we attach to trials of 'porting' between platforms?

There are many different delivery mechanisms for applications nowadays. Software-as-a-service models offer the promise of a lower client-side footprint and a 'use (and pay for) only what you need' culture, and are arguably, therefore, inherently green.

Code reuse is a very good thing in my opinion, but its use has tended primarily to focus on agility rather than performance. So is it really greener to reuse code if you're reusing bloated code?

Systems design principles should mandate that printed reports are produced by exception only, rather than detailed print reports being produced as a matter of course, and ideally we should view more and more system output online.

Procurement – what should we buy and when?

Some procurement decisions are easy, some less so. Old CRT terminals remaining in any part of the business these days are the IT equivalent of a big sign saying *We're not green* and should be managed out of the estate. There is no point any more in ordering a new keyboard, mouse, monitor, cables etc. with a new PC, and there is a point in making sure suppliers deliver PCs with the minimum of packaging.

But when we buy equipment, how long should we expect it to last us before it is greener to replace it than to keep it in operation? A mantra of 'sweat the IT assets as much as you can' is probably greener than one of 'replace computers every three years as soon as we've depreciated the kit', but the best green position is probably somewhere in between.

The issue is not just about the cost of energy to run equipment: it's a case of balancing the locked-in carbon associated with the equipment's manufacture (and taking account of pollutants emitted during production), the supply-chain costs of getting the product to you, the running costs and disposal costs of that equipment, and the same figures for the generation of hardware that will replace it.

One expert's opinion when challenged was that we should be procuring hardware with a view to it lasting us six years or so. Another study presented by DEFRA[5] showed that in a three-year cycle, the manufacture of a PC accounts for approximately 80% of the total energy used, and

---

[5] The study was presented by Bob Crooks of DEFRA at a conference, 'Sustain IT', in London in April 2008, and credits as source 'Eric Williams (UN University, Tokyo) 2005; team analysis'. The screen used in this analysis was a CRT.

furthermore that extending the life of a three-year-old PC by two years (refurbishing it if necessary) would reduce the annual average energy use over the lifetime of the PC by approximately 30%. I've reprinted here, with permission, the latest on the debate about the 'right' time to replace equipment (Source: *Government Computing Magazine,* July 2008):

Catalina McGregor is the Founder and Chair of the CIO CTO Council Green ICT Delivery Sub Group for Her Majesty's Government. She speaks to us upon her return from Brussels where she reports back on the latest green ICT debate:

'Two schools of green ICT thought are emerging and they are deeply conflicted. Some EC Countries firmly believe we should swap out our ICT equipment as soon as possible for more energy efficient equipment to achieve immediate energy savings. And why not? It sounds right, it ticks boxes and produces results for our SOGE targets.

'But is this a false positive?

'Industry have only just begun to provide more energy and resource-efficient solutions, which is a significant leap forward and will be followed no doubt by more efficient software and code. What we are waiting for however is the maths – some scientific studies have shown it's a 3:1 or 6:1 ratio of potential energy savings vs. the carbon footprint for the production of the ICT equipment (depending on the equipment) and that is how many justify the constant "refresh" equipment replacement cycles we are dancing to.

'This is a complex matter and there are many contributing factors but what we will find moving forward is that this ratio will dramatically increase to 15:1 and even 20:1 (depending on the product) as front-end calculations – including mining activity, dynamite blasting, retrieving the metals, transport trucks, transport packing materials, manufacture of parts, welding, manufacturing assembly, toxic materials their extraction and disposal, on-site delivery and finally the end-of-life attempted re-use, recycle and/or disposal figures – come to light.

'The carbon chain is far longer than most CEOs, CIOs and CTOs currently realise as this specialist area is very poorly mapped at this stage. It will be tempting, very tempting to simply go for the "quick fix" and buy new in the coming 3–5 years.

'Fortunately the vast majority of the CIOs and CTOs I know are asking deeper questions but we need to think more carefully about our current equipment and contracts with our industry partners and look to slow down our ICT tech-refresh cycles. Why? Many look at the carbon footprint in China and imagine its not our problem and there isn't much we can do but if they, and other countries, are manufacturing the ICT equipment we are ordering we need to appreciate we are likely to be increasing the carbon footprint output substantially – that is the fundamental risk we are staring at when we say "Green ICT."

'We are expecting a jump in technology both in terms of a reduction of size (preserving scarce resources) and design (snap out replacement an upgrade parts and easier to dismantle parts to enable more efficient re-use and recycling).

'Permanent Secretaries and Ministers have been very supportive of our HMG Green ICT Strategic Vision and we trust those of you who will be reading it in the coming months will understand our approach and seek new appreciation of the total equipment lifecycle challenge we face. Ordering in China, India and any other country is simply that – a new enormous footprint that remains far too unclear and if we are honest we could say we kind of knew that already but we probably didn't realise the magnitude of our procurement decisions from our desks where the day job may simply be to "buy" not to conserve.'

Some companies enforce a 'single PC' policy whereby users are allowed to have a laptop or a desktop but never both, or similarly a mobile phone or a Blackberry but not both. A few companies have gone further and moved to an architecture where users are allowed and even encouraged to use their own PCs as company desktops. There are a number of barriers to such a move, not least issues around data security and equipment support, but these obstacles are being overcome and it is entirely possible that this may be a more common situation in a few years' time.

Going for (EPEAT™) gold

Our PC team experts identify the best models of machine to add to our technology deployment roadmap, and earlier this year they happily took up the challenge to introduce a more energy-efficient PC as our standard device. We'll deploy this in our newest department store in Leicester when that opens at the end of summer 2008, and other areas of the business will follow suit when new PCs are required (and we definitely mean required, not just desired!).

The team are now recommending the first Intel-based desktop from our supplier, Lenovo, to have a gold EPEAT rating (Electronic Product Environmental Assessment Tool[6]). The machine is also Energy Star 4.0 compliant[7], a measure of its energy efficiency across all modes of the computer's operation, ensuring energy savings when a computer is active and running basic applications, as well as in low power modes.

The special bid price we agreed for this model was a little more expensive than the previous standard. However, we

---

[6] http://www.epeat.net 'EPEAT is a system to help purchasers in the public and private sectors evaluate, compare and select desktop computers, notebooks and monitors based on their environmental attributes. EPEAT also provides a clear and consistent set of performance criteria for the design of products, and provides an opportunity for manufacturers to secure market recognition for efforts to reduce the environmental impact of its products.'

[7] http://www.energystar.gov 'ENERGY STAR is a joint program of the US Environmental Protection Agency and the US Department of Energy helping us all save money and protect the environment through energy efficient products and practices.'

calculated that the savings to be made from the lower power consumption will far outweigh the additional cost associated with the device.

Although we haven't encountered it as an issue, it's always possible that resistance to such a choice of standard model might come from stakeholders who 'don't like that model'. But then this isn't a green issue as such, more an issue in general of how enterprise standards are agreed and enforced.

Remember that the EPEAT standard is designed to evolve and improve such that this year's gold model might only be rated silver or bronze in future years. Thus a commitment to EPEAT gold means keeping the marketplace under review and tracking the standard for new purchases.

Use – a green storage war on terabytes

At John Lewis we have had a storage area network (SAN) since late 2004. It is a virtualised environment, and is itself an enabler for server virtualisation, which is discussed later in the book.

We've seen a phenomenal growth in the demand for storage capacity in the past few years. In 2004 we started with 8 terabytes of capacity – by May 2008 we had about 30 times as much! This significantly outstrips the data capacity growth we've been used to seeing over the past 20 years, which was a doubling in capacity every 18 months or so. That in itself had sometimes seemed a relentless rise. The current, almost hyperinflationary, demand for application storage has been scary and it remains to be seen whether this trend will continue for a few years or whether we will see the tailing off of an S curve. Either way, all of this data needs an infrastructure to support it, and it is one that has a carbon footprint.

Any discussion of greening storage infrastructures should begin with the statement that the greenest form of storage possible for a terabyte of data is *not needing to store that terabyte at all.* Managing demand is particularly important because studies (source – Sun) have shown that 70% or so of data held on corporate SANs is not needed.

We are only just getting to grips at JLP with this topic and reining in demand for extra storage capacity is one that will depend on a variety of techniques. One such approach is the use of a 'deduplication' technology to remove identical copies of the same data from the environment.[8] In preparing departmental PowerPoint presentations I'm often struck by how many similar versions of the same presentation exist on my own laptop hard drive, and application systems also often keep copies that are not needed. A green agenda (and other drivers too, such as compliance) should drive the formalisation of companies' data retention and archiving strategies, and we shouldn't forget the role to be played in this by poor old unfashionable tape, a form of storage that is inherently greener in its energy use than disk.

Charging departments fairly for the storage they are using is one way to drive behaviour change so that systems only use and pay for the storage they need; but the ability to do this of course depends on the sophistication of the SAN management software in providing that usage data.

---

[8] Often called 'intelligent compression' or 'single-instance storage', this is a method of reducing storage needs by eliminating redundant data. Only one unique instance of the data is actually retained. Redundant data is replaced with a pointer to the unique data copy.

Implementing a hierarchy of SAN storage infrastructure layers can help us ensure that we aren't providing expensive storage for application data when for some of it a cheaper and greener infrastructure layer would suffice.

Sleepy disk drives and MAIDs

Sleepy drives can perhaps be regarded as a new 'low-end' storage tier suitable for some applications. They have however not yet proved popular. There's energy to be saved by 'spinning down' inactive disk drives to reduce power consumption (and also now heat generation), but there is a hefty performance penalty to pay (in the time it takes to wake a sleepy drive), and as a result there have been few takers. As energy prices rise, this technology area may start to see more activity. The concept is actually not a new one, and has been used in laptop computers for quite a while now, to extend battery life, but it has only recently started to be used in SANs.

A massive array of idle disks (MAID) is slightly different – it shuts down a large proportion of drives when they are not in active use. MAIDs have been designed specifically to never spin more than a fraction of their disk drives (about 25% maximum) at any one moment. Far less power is therefore consumed inside a MAID array, and far less heat generated.

However, shutting down electronic circuits can reduce drive life, because of the voltage surges that can occur when power is switched back on. MAID technology needs to mature and overcome obstacles like this to stand a realistic chance of reaching mainstream adoption.

Within the John Lewis Partnership we have no plans currently to examine these new technology areas, and we will concentrate instead on maturing our storage infrastructure and management processes further and then turn our efforts to managing demand and decelerating capacity growth using deduplication technology.

Disposal

For over five years, JLP has worked with a supplier for the recycling of our redundant IT equipment. The arrangement exceeds all UK and European recycling legislation (WEEE directive), and we can also boast 'zero per cent landfill'.

We are aware that life has moved on since we put these disposal arrangements in place and so we keep this arrangement under review and discuss alternative reuse and recycling options with the incumbent supplier and with others. We are cautious, though, to ensure that we do not enter into an arrangement which might result in us simply shifting our company's IT disposal problem to the Third World.

Some of our suppliers also provide us with a means of recycling hardware, for example used toner cartridges. And we are part of a trade-in programme for redundant networking equipment which ensures the equipment is either recycled, given an extended life elsewhere or disposed of responsibly.

One company I spoke to recently recommended visiting your recycling or reuse supplier unannounced, and asking to see your equipment for the disposal of which they are responsible. You should then get an immediate sense of how confident in their capability you can continue to be, simply by their ability to deal with such an unheralded request.

The largest relevant body in Government is the Ministry of Defence Disposals Service Authority (DSA). They assure market value is obtained on public purse expenditure rather than simply returning used goods to suppliers for no returns. Often called 'the green sandals brigade', the DSA can assess any items a government department wishes to re-use, re-sell or recycle. This includes office furniture, Green IT, phones, video equipment, desktops, laptops, any textiles (even used socks!), ships, vehicles and all sorts of base materials in case a building is being destroyed. The MOD also has a Green IT 'eBay-style' website where many government items are for sale – see www.edisposals.com.

CHAPTER 5: ENGAGING WITH EMPLOYEES

We found from the start of our Green IT work that an overwhelming majority of colleagues, both within and outside the IT department, were highly supportive of these initiatives, happy to do what they could to help, and able to translate that support into practical action. It may be that we're a lot luckier than most, since the John Lewis Partnership is an employee-owned retail business, very conscious of the need to only use what we need. (When I joined the company in 1989, one of the first things I noticed was stickers underneath the light switches with *Switch Off! You're Burning our Bonus!* printed on them.)

However, I suspect that we're not alone and that the atmosphere in most firms is well-disposed towards such work. In the closing years of the first decade of the 21st century there is a palpable desire among many employees to *do the right thing* to help fight climate change, even if this means abandoning past practices and learning to adapt to a different world. This may not be a permanent phenomenon, of course, and disillusionment is likely if we don't capitalise effectively on this period of goodwill towards change.

Some stereotypes

Despite such goodwill, every now and then you may come across a character in your IT organisation or outside it who falls into one of the following (exaggerated) categories:

- **Rubbishers:** those who still don't believe the science despite (or possibly even because of) the general consensus.
- **Happy fatalists:** those who believe the science but figure, *We're all doomed anyway now, so what's the point?*
- **Distracted evangelists:** enthusiasts so keen to save the world that they will charge ahead with the first Green IT action that might help without even stopping to consider whether it's actually green or the most effective one to choose.
- **Angel-on-pinhead counters:** the opposite extreme, folk who will debate endlessly the contrasting green merits of alternate courses of action.

The point of this digression into stereotyping of behaviours is that if you do encounter any of these attitudes, it's worth pausing and asking yourself what response you are seeking from the people concerned, and what techniques you will use to best influence that.

For example, you don't need to attempt to convert a rubbisher before making use of their expertise to solve a particular problem, and they'll willingly give you that help. Happy fatalists will usually cheer up over a glass of wine if you make sure you celebrate success as green initiatives are implemented. Techniques like the acorns diagram described earlier can help bring the distracted evangelists back on track. The angel counters can help the cause if you task them with defining the calculations needed to answer the *Which is best?* questions, while also reminding them of the need for urgency.

Making it easier to do the right thing

When it comes to users (and it's worth remembering that we're all users of IT, of course), there is undeniably more that we in IT departments can do to help nurture good green behaviour across our organisations. To a certain extent, this is simply a case of making sure that green behaviours which employees have become used to adopting at home are also observed in the office.

For example, help users to better understand the impact of their actions in, say, printing 20 copies of a 100-page report by putting a sign above each printer showing them the cost of each page printed. The trick is to get employees to adopt alternative behaviours which don't significantly detract from the outcome from their point of view (get them to use double-sided printing as a matter of course, perhaps), but which produce less of a negative impact.

If you can go further, of course, and automate the IT such that they actively have to choose if they want to take the action with the greater carbon footprint (e.g. users will get double-sided print unless they override the setting manually, and are presented with an *Are you sure?* message) then even better.

Consider using events such as World Environment Day each year to kickstart your message. Some excerpts from the Global Action Plan study *An Inefficient Truth* give some useful pointers here:

Individual employees have control over many ICT decisions during their daily work, such as whether to turn off equipment, print documents or save files and e-mails, which all have energy implications.

...whether an organisation decides to allow staff wide authority over their own working practices or not, few organisations currently have considerable control over most of their employee's decisions which affect the environment. Staff engagement on environmental issues remains a key factor in workplace efficiency and when companies take on the challenge of encouraging good environmental practice, then employees, their families and the community will benefit.

Global Action Plan has run a staff engagement programme called 'Environment Champions' for the past decade, and has helped organisations to reduce the amount of energy wasted by IT equipment:

In this programme, groups of volunteer employees identify areas of energy wastage before running a communication campaign to encourage their colleagues to practice more efficient behaviour.

One such group of Champions was established by Construction Skills in 2006 (then the Construction Industry Training Board). The Champions worked out that whilst their colleagues were quite efficient, the 10% of computers and 24% of monitors that were left on over lunch and out of hours were wasting around 26,000 kWh and £2,000 of energy, and emitting 14 tonnes of CO_2 each year. Out of the 900 users, this level of energy waste was not excessive, but the Champions thought their colleagues could do better and set about the tricky task of changing behaviour.

The Champions calculated the emissions from leaving one monitor on for an hour (about 40 litres of CO_2) and illustrated this, by tying bunches of 8 party balloons to a selection of monitors around the site. This visual representation was coupled with the instigation of a league *of energy-wasting departments. In random energy spot checks, Champions left green stickers on equipment turned off and put red stickers on equipment turned on. This friendly competition particularly inspired managers who rigorously promoted energy efficiency to their teams to avoid coming bottom of the league.*

At JLP we have what a colleague calls the 'Santa Claus report', a league-table measure of the energy consumption by each JLP department store in the early hours of Christmas Day morning, the idea being that that day gives us the fairest measure of which branches are most diligently switching off equipment that doesn't need to be on overnight or at weekends.

Innovative ideas from employees

When canvassing for ideas on greening IT (and I'd recommend doing this in your companies to supplement the suggestions presented in this book and elsewhere), always try and remember that no one team, department or job function has the monopoly on good ideas. Some of the best ideas for positive change can come from those who aren't necessarily the acknowledged subject experts. Asked the right questions, employees are very capable of coming up with ideas to improve their business, whether these are incremental (continuous improvement), innovations or even more radical ideas for change.

Of course, innovation, and in particular the opportunity for more open innovation facilitated by Web 2.0 technologies, is itself another hot topic in IT currently. The IT department's opportunity to help is not just through IT innovation itself but also by providing a framework (tools and processes) which will enable and support a more innovative corporate culture. Social networking software offers the potential to improve our ability to assess, filter and progress innovative ideas, by using the best aspects of 'wikis' and online communities. I can't think of a better problem area to try this new muscle out against than energy consumption.

Some companies such as Proctor and Gamble have even gone so far as to use open innovation web sites (sometimes referred to as 'eBays for ideas') such as www.innocentive.com and www.ninesigma.com to solve thorny business problems, and maybe this will also be a means to help identify the next generation of Green IT solutions.

We take for granted in the IT world that it's always very hard to get a business case accepted. In part, I think that can be down to our discipline's inability to communicate benefits effectively to the rest of the business. But it is worth remembering that a positive green impact can be a powerful business driver for change. Of course, you should always be entirely truthful about any green benefits you are claiming (to not do so would not only be immoral but also ultimately self-defeating). And you'll still need to make your case. But don't underestimate your companies' appetites for innovative ways to demonstrate their green credentials.

CHAPTER 6: THE CHALLENGE TO SUPPLIERS

As discussed earlier, it's only natural to be cynical of the motives of some IT suppliers when it comes to Green IT. I feel that there has been perhaps a little too much of a backlash against 'greenwash', 'green froth', call it what you will. Snake-oil salesmen undoubtedly exist in IT and always will, but it's equally true that some IT suppliers are doing great work and it makes very good sense to engage with them on the topic.

Once a year at the John Lewis Partnership the Directors responsible for IT host an event for 50 account managers, representing our key IT suppliers, bringing them together in one place for a day. And tempting though it might sometimes be to get them in the room, lock the door, head back to the office and get on with our jobs safe from salespeople for another year, we actually feel JLP benefits hugely from working with them in this way.

At this event, the suppliers get to hear about our plans and strategy as a company and about how IT is supporting that (but what we are happy to share with them and no more, of course). We remind them what behaviours we expect of them as suppliers and give them a better idea of how they can help us meet our objectives for the coming year.

By sharing information in this way we don't necessarily end up spending less time with our suppliers during the year, but we do increase the quality of the relationships we have with them and the consistency of the message to that community about what is important to us in our dealings with IT suppliers.

The IT supplier day is an obvious opportunity to include a discussion of our green agenda with them, and that is indeed what we have done for the last couple of years. The challenges we make are different from year to year but include the following:

What are you doing to enable/support Green IT within your own organisations?

What are you doing to enable/support Green IT in your dealings with your own suppliers?

What are you doing to enable/support Green IT in the hardware, software and services you supply to us? (For example, are you 'choice-editing' your product range?)

What are you doing to make sure that you're speaking the same 'language' (green standards etc.) to us as the other suppliers here?

What are you doing to ensure your products are certified to work in a virtualised environment?

What are you doing to improve software licensing models to more fairly reflect a virtualised world?

How are you helping us to avoid what we might term 'upgrade-itis', the seemingly constant need to replace or add to our hardware estate with newer models to support your software?

What are the green initiatives we may not have thought of that you believe the Partnership should be pursuing, and how can you help us progress those?

Why are you sending us all these boxes of software licence documentation?

The last of these challenges (*see photo*) was included so we could have some gentle fun at a particular supplier's expense, but there was a serious point behind it too, and of course, sometimes with Green IT, it is visible issues like this that can really impact a supplier's perceived green credentials.

The background to the story is that we had received in 2007 a delivery of a large number of boxes each containing 10 full shrink-wrapped boxed copies of a well-known operating system, these being required to licence part of our John Lewis branch terminal estate. At the time we had approximately 2100 such terminals, about 100 per branch, so that's 210 separate boxes of licence documentation.

Because we install the operating systems from an image, all of these boxes will remain unopened (or at best flat-packed for storage), only being kept because we are required to keep the original box, CD (with licence key), manuals and invoice (receipt) as proof or purchase.

To be fair, most of our licences from that vendor are purchased electronically (and we keep invoices as proof of purchase) via an overall licence agreement but unfortunately these copies fell outside of this scheme as they were administered by another division of the supplier organisation.

Badbuster

The Badbuster browser plug-in – see www.badbuster.com – is a possible sign of things to come, and if you haven't used it before, I'd encourage you to take a look. It automatically rates companies (US-based only at launch) on their green credentials and highlights the company name with a red, amber or green underline based on aggregate results of independent green assessments of that company. The tool is relatively unsophisticated in its assessment methodology, but this will improve I am sure, and it shows how the scores are calculated.

Tendering documents

Requests for Information (RFIs) or Requests for Proposals (RFPs) are sent to suppliers when we are procuring hardware, software or services for a large IT project and need to ask questions which will help us choose between more than one supplier.

It makes sense to incorporate a 'Green IT' section within an RFI/RFP using standard language expressing our desire to purchase environmentally preferable products and services. A few months ago I put together a standard template for such a section based on the standards I was aware of and RFP elements I could see online that other organisations[9] were already asking suppliers, and I reproduce that here.

It is relatively new at JLP and has only been used by a couple of our projects so far. What I'd like to see released is a more sophisticated cross-industry template available for

---

[9] In particular my thanks go to the Northwest Product Stewardship Council in the United States at www.productstewardship.net

companies such as ours to use, so that we can ask suppliers these questions in a standard format (on the basis that we're all facing similar issues, and that the suppliers are more likely to spend the time answering these questions properly and taking action to improve their credentials if asked the same questions in a consistent and repeated manner). This is also an area that the Enterprise IT Leadership Team have expressed an interest in taking forward, and one on which Catalina McGregor of the MOD and colleagues have already done some fine work

Compliance with environmental legislation and industry standards

- To what extent do you comply with the environmental performance standard for electronic products – IEEE 1680 – as summarised on the EPEAT website (see www.epeat.net) standards including their extension to other products such as imaging devices?
- To what extent do you meet the WEEE directive, as summarised at www.berr.gov.uk/? How is this audited and certified?
- To what extent do you meet the ROHS directive, as summarised at www.rohs.gov.uk/ ? How is this audited and certified?
- To what extent do you meet Energy Star compliance, as described at www.energystar.gov?

Obsolescence versus upgradability

Planned obsolescence and design-for-disposal uses up natural resources and causes waste.

- Do you offer lease and take-back options? Please give details.
- Please give details as to the how easily the software you provide can be upgraded. What is the process involved?
- Please give details as to how easily the hardware you provide (including memory) can be upgraded. What is the process involved?
- Please indicate how you will make sure relevant spare parts and service are available (define this in 'years available after production').

Packaging and shipping of computer equipment

Computer equipment comes packaged in materials that typically cannot be reused, separated or recycled. Glued computer parts and multiple-material packaging impede recycling. Materials such as polystyrene are generally made without recycled content and may be non-recyclable. Excessive packaging is wasteful. Paper manuals and disks packaged with each computer often add to the waste.

- Do you package computer units together when shipping rather than boxing individually? Please give details.
- To what extent do you use recycled-content materials and recyclable packaging? How many different types of materials are used?
- Are those material types which can be recycled clearly labelled as such (type of plastic, metal, etc.)?
- Do you offer a service whereby you take back packaging for reuse or recycling? Please give details.
- Do you provide on-line rather than paper-based manuals?

Toxic materials

Manufacturing of computers and component parts typically involves solvents and other substances that must be controlled to reduce pollution and health risks. Cadmium, mercury, lead and brominated or halogenated compounds do not break down readily in nature, and require special management.

- What levels of the following toxic chemicals do you use during manufacturing and assembly?
  - CFCs or HCFCs
  - chlorinated solvents
  - cadmium
  - mercury
  - chlorinated or brominated flame retardants.
- Do you offer take-back provisions for all equipment including such materials.
- Do you use lead-free solder?
- Where glass is used, have you used glass-to-glass recycling as part of your manufacturing process?
- Do you use only low-mercury and long-life lamps in flat panel displays?
- Are all batteries supplied by you removable, rechargeable, and recyclable?
- Do you label battery type and weight, and give instructions for recycling, removal and installation?

Other design and manufacturing factors, including printing-related issues

Product design and manufacturing should address air and water pollution and employee health concerns. Virgin and non-recyclable materials use up more water, energy and minerals than recycled materials.

- Do you use products and parts designed so they can be disassembled with universally available tools; minimise use of fasteners, e.g. 'snap-in, snap-out' assembly?
- Do you use readily recyclable metal casings? Metal rather than plastic housings in some products can eliminate the need for halogenated flame retardants and increase recyclability.
- Do you use recycled-content materials, remanufactured or refurbished equipment? Please give details.
- How do you minimise the toxicity and variety of adhesives, labels, coatings, finishes, fasteners and metallic paints?
- How will you allow us to automatically enforce such policies such as 'duplex as standard' and 'double-sided as standard' printing?
- Do you use remanufactured toner cartridges?
- Please give the air quality standards your printers meet, e.g. ozone concentration and dust concentration (expressed in mg/m^3 and/or mg/hour determined in full operation of the product).

CHAPTER 7: GREEN SERVERS – VIRTUALISATION

Of the Green IT projects we took forward within the John Lewis Partnership, this was the earliest big success. The right environmental course of action was also shown to be an excellent one commercially. We were shortlisted by *Computing* magazine for their 'Green IT project of the year' award in 2007 for this work.

Recognising the need

Like most IT departments, we need to devote much of our time on projects and tasks to keeping the lights on. However, we also have a regular forum of technical architects which tracks emerging and maturing technologies and helps steer our IT strategy, and in late 2006 there was a growing recognition by that group that what might be termed 'perfect storm' conditions (to borrow Gartner's term) were gathering over our Intel server estate:

- Although we had reduced our server space requirements by consolidating onto blade centres, we faced some real concerns about power, cooling and floor space, particularly in our secondary datacentre facility at Victoria.
- Our projections showed likely demand for new servers continuing to increase, while at the same time very few old servers were being decommissioned. We knew that if we did nothing we would need to lease additional datacentre space, at short notice and considerable cost.

- Moore's Law[10] had cast a long shadow over JLP's use of hardware. Increasingly powerful commodity Intel servers were in operation, but these were running at progressively lower utilisation levels – we surveyed this and found that the average figure was 8% utilisation.

We were tracking developments in the server virtualisation product marketplace, so we knew we had to act. We could see that server virtualisation products were starting to show a step change in maturity, with VMware's new version of its software leading the field (see www.vmware.com/products/server_virtualization.html). We decided to undertake a four-week size-of-the-prize exercise with that vendor to see what sort of consolidation ratio we might expect if we were to adopt widespread server virtualisation.

The results were significant: even the most cautious interpretation of this study's findings showed a 10 to 1 or even 12 to 1 projected ratio of virtual to physical servers would be possible. As news of that spread across the IT department, we then found at every governance step that we were pushing at an open door with our proposal to proceed with a proper pilot in early 2007.

In 2004 we had already implemented a storage area network (SAN), which had demonstrated the available efficiencies in meeting demand for storage through virtualisation and paved the way for server virtualisation.

[10] Moore's Law in 1965 stated that the number of transistors per square inch on a chip will double roughly every two years. The current definition (sanctioned by Moore) is that the density will double every 18 months.

Making it happen

We did ourselves a big favour by bringing in as a project manager for this work an experienced member of the department with a background of many years' operational support.

We installed five large IBM xSeries servers, initially to support a pilot of only 20 virtual servers, but the pilot was immediately successful to the point that we had virtualised nearly 60 servers within a few weeks. And we had soon taken the decision that nearly all new server requirements, with immediate effect, would be provisioned as virtualised servers. (Lotus Notes and SQL server infrastructures remain the notable exceptions because of their I/O needs. They're not exempt, though, and the teams are responding to the challenge to physically consolidate those computing environments in other ways.)

These 60 were a mixture of test and production servers, new requirements and existing server cutovers, and during the pilot we also virtualised servers belonging to different teams. We had deliberately chosen not just to go for the easy option.

Nevertheless, through the virtualisation of just these pilot servers, we were able to demonstrate savings of over £100,000 in new server purchases, 120U of rack space, 1.5 metric tonnes in weight, numerous network and SAN connections and £8,000 in consumed power, plus of course associated air-conditioning savings – in only a couple of months.

Our customers soon appreciated our new ability to provision a new server in an elapsed time of under an hour rather than weeks, and the project showed that we could free up PC team members' time and allow them to perform higher-value tasks.

At this stage there was a real temptation to press ahead and virtualise the remaining servers as soon as possible. But we had from the outset been mindful that the hardest challenge would not be in implementation but in ongoing management of this new infrastructure. The VMware product itself had some impressive management utilities, but we knew from experience of managing other environments that software in itself would not suffice. We had therefore agreed in advance to take a three-month break from further migrations after the pilot, from April to July 2007, and we spent this time consulting all affected operational, service management, application system and technical infrastructure teams, in order to put together all of the processes we felt were necessary to proceed with a near-wholesale migration to a virtualised estate.

This was time very well spent. We ensured that we had settled on our processes and procedures (generally based on the ITIL framework) for capacity forecasting and provisioning, internal charging for the new environment (with tariffs to make it easiest for application teams to choose the green option) and change management. We agreed how proactive monitoring and problem management of the estate would happen, how we'd ensure high availability and allow for proper business continuity tests.

And we ensured that ethical disposal of old servers was covered too. As part of this consultation exercise we raised awareness of this project and of green issues generally across our IT department and were very pleased with how thoroughly teams all bought in to what we were doing.

We used some gimmicks to communicate the benefits as part of this awareness exercise – for example to show how the power saved equated to that used by a growing number of homes in the neighbourhood of the project manager (thanks to Google maps!) and to show what the floor loading of server weight we had avoided equated to (*see photos*).

We then started the next phase of work, growing our estate to 22 physical VMware hosts, onto which we are migrating an increasing proportion of our existing server base. We have a target of 200 server migrations before our next scheduled pause when we will review, reflect and replan as necessary. Our aim is to reach a milestone over the next year when more than half of our entire estate of Intel servers is virtualised.

Desktop virtualisation

Having virtualised servers and storage before that, the next environment for us to consider is the desktop, and we are currently evaluating solutions for desktop virtualisation to determine whether there is a case for us to do that too.

Some companies have done this successfully already and indeed the *Inefficient Truth* report has a very good case study on the replacement of traditional desktop PCs with thin clients, which I've reproduced here with permission.

Reed Managed Services (Reed) is a high street recruitment agency that operates over 300 retail branches in the UK. Reed's worldwide IT estate encompasses over 4,500 PCs and 400 laptops, plus around 300 servers hosting data across the entire network.

Reed found that many servers were not being used to their full capacity. In addition, servers and desktop computers were generating significant heat which needed to be removed through air-conditioning, both in the workplace areas and the datacentre.

As well as striving to reduce its carbon footprint, Reed's target was to make its IT infrastructure more cost efficient, and to ensure the ongoing security and effective management of its data to meet business and data protection requirements.

Reed explored the possibility of using thin computing, whereby applications and data could be centrally hosted and delivered to thin-client terminals across both local and wide area networks.

A number of considerations had to be taken into account:

- the actual terminals must be capable of fast processing speeds;
- the need to manage the emerging protocols, standards, patches and hardware effectively and efficiently;
- it must be flexible enough to adapt to any economic changes.

Reed decided to trial thin-client terminals provided by Wyse Technology over a period of three months. The trial demonstrated to the board that the solution was easy to set up and manage, in addition to being economic and environmentally friendly to run.

The trial also proved a real success amongst the end users. Those on the trial could work remotely in a way that had not been previously possible. Using a small security device, they could securely log into a session regardless of their location. They could also access all files and programs from any workstation, whether they were working from home or from another office, without going through complicated logon and networking procedures.

The thin computing model also gave Reed's staff the opportunity to implement greener working practices in their day-to-day routines. Due to the daily need to update PCs with anti-virus definitions plus frequent operating system patches, the existing PCs were being left on 24 hours a day so this management could take place out-of-hours.

With the thin clients the need for desktop patching was greatly reduced, and changes could be applied using the Wyse management software. The fast start-up time of the terminals also enabled Reed to encourage staff to switch off at lunchtime and the end of the working day.

Reed replaced all of its 4,500 PCs over a period of just 10 weeks, which significantly minimised disruption during implementation.

In order to maximise its investment in the new thin terminals, Reed reviewed its entire infrastructure. They invested in blade servers in its datacentre, which were selected both for performance and for power efficiency. They were able to optimise the power efficiency of its server infrastructure by de-commissioning servers in remote offices and by using server virtualisation technology in the data centre to achieve high server utilisation levels. In turn, this reduced air-conditioning requirements. Reed has also reduced the amount of energy used for cooling in its datacentres as air conditioning was previously set at an unnecessarily low temperature.

With servers in the datacentre running all the time, Reed was keen to fully maximise utilisation. The thin computing approach enables computing services to be delivered to users anywhere in the world, so the same servers are now used to deliver desktop computing to users abroad at times when the servers would otherwise be standing idle. As well as being energy efficient, this flexible infrastructure means Reed can very rapidly set up new offices as business requirements change. For example, in Australia they were able to setup up a remote office in just four weeks.

Within a year of switching to a thin computing model, Reed had achieved its goal of significantly reducing its carbon footprint. They have seen a reduction in energy consumption of approximately 5.4 million kWh of power – that's 2,800 tonnes of CO_2 per annum. Combined with halving the number of storage drives and reducing the number of servers by a factor of 20, Reed's annual IT budget has been reduced by a fifth.

CHAPTER 8: GREEN PRINTING

Paper is far more expensive than the printing process, consuming 10 times the energy, according to Gartner.[11] The issue for most companies, therefore, is the volume of printing (Gartner also reckon that a typical office worker prints 1,000 pages a month). The 'paperless office' never really happened, and it seems that all we really managed instead is 'transient paper', where we still all print a lot but just don't keep the evidence. There is also the issue of the sheer number of printing devices a company has – usually significantly more than it needs.

Moving to a managed print service

In 2007 we embarked on a review which ultimately recommended the introduction of a managed print service to replace the existing approach to document output facilities in our Victoria head office buildings.

Within the scope of the project were standard office printers, photocopiers, faxes and scanners. The relatively small number of specialist printers such as large format plotters were excluded.

The review we conducted highlighted the inefficiencies in our situation and recommended we move to a document output infrastructure with a single point of control and effective management information.

---

[11] Gartner report: '10 Key Elements of a "Green IT" Strategy', 7 December 2007, available from www.gartner.com

Specific issues we needed to address

We had a situation where multiple contracts, with different cycles, and a mix of leased and purchased equipment, were being managed by a number of different people within different teams across our organisation

No single team owned printing in the head office building, which meant that there was no overview or management control. We had no accurate account of what equipment we had, where it was, who was using it or what volumes were produced (and what they cost). When we conducted an exercise to gather the data to tell us this we could produce a point-in-time snapshot at considerable effort, but we had no easy means of maintaining it and it was soon out of date.

The review showed that the vast majority of our printers – which are depreciated over 3 years – were over 3-years old; in fact 40% were more than 5-years old with at least one as much as 10-years old!

Our printers averaged 3.1 service calls each year, whereas modern laser printers should average only 0.25 calls. They were old and energy-inefficient.

The way that devices were bought and depreciated from a number of different directorate budgets had led to an excessive number of devices, many of which were over- or under-specified for the type and volume of printing produced from them.

The photocopiers on the estate were considered old and unreliable, requiring interventions from both general office users and support staff to keep them going.

Scanners were purchased as required. Because we had not networked these devices yet, more and more devices were being locally attached to individual PCs as demand for the facility increases.

Some equipment was covered by a general hardware maintenance contract and some was not.

We generally relied on a directorate secretary, or other nominated individual, to take responsibility for ordering paper, toner and other print consumables for their department. General office users tended to replace paper and toner cartridges once the device has ceased to work. They also placed calls to the appropriate helpdesk to report faults on printers, monochrome photocopiers, faxes and scanners.

The review suggested that we could achieve an improvement in the number of people accessing each printer from the average of 4.7 to a healthier figure of 12.7.

Supplier selection

We agreed to tender during 2007 for a managed print service contract. We issued a request for information and the subsequent responses enabled us to reduce our potential provider list to four suppliers:

- our incumbent hardware manufacturer
- a market-leading print device manufacturer
- our incumbent (multi-vendor) hardware maintenance provider
- an alternative multivendor print service provider.

A project working group completed site and reference visits for each of the potential providers and then scored their responses to the tender document. We ultimately selected a solution involving two of the vendors (the print device manufacturer and incumbent hardware maintenance provider) working together which we felt gave us the best of both worlds.

This move to a managed print service was not primarily driven by cost savings. However, the new environment, once fully rolled out (and following a successful pilot which is underway as I write in June 2008), will have enabled us to make real cost savings. In addition, we will have greatly improved the efficiency of the service. It will streamline the supply chain and provide us with the tools to start actively managing the costs of printing on the estate.

Benefits

It is this element that was the main driver for change, because with ongoing management information, we can now start to properly keep track of printing costs, and begin to successfully drive them down, with the associated green benefits of less paper, cartridges and energy used. (*If you can't measure, you can't manage.*) The management software associated with the solution we plumped for will be able to support a potential move we might make to implement charge-back of print costs to departments.

There are other options under consideration such as 'follow me' printing, a piece of software that enables users to retrieve their print jobs from any printer on the estate – useful if we increase hot-desking. It can help to eliminate waste paper left beside printers, as no job is printed unless the user is there to call it off.

Printers have now become officially part of the head office building's IT infrastructure and are sourced from a single budget.

Think before you print!

Linked to this project has been a publicity exercise for head office users to make them aware of printing costs. Figure 6 shows one of the posters we display next to the printers. We have different posters for different printer models to educate staff on the cheapest and greenest printers to use.

Figure 6: Staff education

CHAPTER 9: GREEN DESKTOPS – POWER MANAGEMENT

This section describes some technologies and techniques for reducing the power used by desktops. Please bear in mind throughout, though, that a PC that has been turned off still consumes some energy: it needs to be unplugged to not use power.

Wake-on-LAN software

In 2007 and unrelated to our green work, one of our teams was evaluating products for patch management as an add-on to the Microsoft System Management Server (SMS) software which we use to manage our desktop PC estate.

Two products, SMSWakeup and NightWatchman, make up the patch management solution from a company called 1E.[12] The products function independently of each other. While our initial focus was providing an effective out-of-hours patching and software deployment tool (SMSWakeup's functionality), we soon realised that there were some hefty savings (£100,000 per annum) that could be realised if all devices were to be turned off at night by NightWatchman, a power management solution to automate PC shutdown and control Windows power schema via Group Policy. Figure 7 shows the expected savings.

We embarked on pilots in a John Lewis branch (Kingston) and at our Victoria and Bracknell head offices, and verified

---

[12] www.1e.com

that the products worked well, We determined that just under a third of PC devices were being left on overnight across the company, and agreed to proceed with a rollout which is underway now to nearly all of John Lewis Partnership desktops, including some point-of-sale register PCs.

Estimate the daily cost savings that can be made using NightWatchman to shut down computers earlier

Date	Original (KWh)	Proposed (KWh)	Saving (KWh)	Original Cost	Proposed Cost	Saving Cost
20/10/2007	7132.09	5152	1980.09	£534.91	£386.40	£148.51
21/10/2007	5975.86	4094.91	1880.94	£448.19	£307.12	£141.07
22/10/2007	9529.03	7510.05	2018.98	£714.68	£563.25	£151.42
23/10/2007	9941.28	7835.28	2106	£745.60	£587.65	£157.95
24/10/2007	9982.91	7895.9	2087.02	£748.72	£592.19	£156.53
25/10/2007	9959.73	7852.38	2107.35	£746.98	£588.93	£158.05
26/10/2007	9423.39	7355.25	2068.14	£706.75	£551.64	£155.11
27/10/2007	6843.95	4947.85	1896.1	£513.30	£371.09	£142.21
28/10/2007	5803.74	3984.14	1819.6	£435.28	£298.81	£136.47
29/10/2007	9545.62	7587.53	1958.09	£715.92	£569.06	£146.86
30/10/2007	10745.45	8245.56	2499.89	£805.91	£618.42	£187.49
31/10/2007	11218.87	8404.19	2814.68	£841.41	£630.31	£211.10
01/11/2007	11246.46	8461.76	2784.7	£843.48	£634.63	£208.85
02/11/2007	9630.04	7409.09	2220.94	£722.25	£555.68	£166.57
Total:	**126978.42**	**96735.89**	**30242.52**	**£9,523.38**	**£7,255.18**	**£2,268.19**

Figure 7: Power savings estimator, daily

The product works by having a client-side agent installed on all of the computers we want to manage. The NightWatchman agent was designed to work in isolation on each device, with users able to stop or suspend shutdown for twenty-four hours. The software tries to save any open documents and aborts the shutdown if this is not possible.

We had some initial concerns about the automated shutting down of our Lotus Notes mail software. To address this 1E provided us with a Notes shutdown script tailored to our environment.

Nightwatchman software monitors the operating system for any power state changes and can report this information back to us across the network, giving us the metrics we need to see exactly how much the desktop environment is costing us in electricity consumption.

We're now starting to realise some significant savings as a result of our use of the product.

Other power management initiatives

We're also beginning a trial of a product called the Ecobutton™.[13] It is a USB-connected device, essentially a large button that users can press whenever they leave their desks to instantly place their computer into a low-power standby mode, as opposed to a more power-hungry standby mode, which most desktops computers are set to use it is claimed. When they return to their desks they simply need to press any key on the keyboard and the PC is instantly woken up again. It's a lot greener than using a screen-saver!

The device comes with software to show users how much power and therefore carbon and money they have saved by using it. It is made from recycled plastic (and is RoHS[14] compliant). Although it works for both desktops and laptops, we understand that the advantage in using it for laptops is negligible given that they also use level 3 standby mode.

We plan also to evaluate other devices or techniques that reduce power even further when a computer shuts down, in the hope of getting our power consumption as low as we can. The policy of turning off what we don't need extends to the LCD displays on our head office telephones, which are all set to automatically switch off in the evening and

---

[13] www.eco-button.com

[14] The Directive on the Restriction of the Use of Certain Hazardous Substances in Electrical and Electronic Equipment 2002/95/EC[1] (commonly referred to as the Restriction of Hazardous Substances Directive or RoHS). See www.rohs.gov.uk.

back on again in the morning to reduce energy consumption.

CHAPTER 10: DATACENTRE ENVIRONMENTAL CONSIDERATIONS

Staying on the previous chapter's subject of power consumption costs, our main datacentre at Bracknell costs us £265,000 per annum, and our secondary computer room facility at the Victoria head office takes that up to a combined annual power cost for both datacentres of approximately £330,000.

Who pays the bills?

IT is clearly a major user of electricity, but very few IT departments (including us) pay their own electricity bill directly. There is a resultant danger that IT purchasing decisions can be made as though we were 'buying a car knowing someone else will pay for the petrol' (comment taken from *ITWeek*, 12 March 2007).

Some IT departments choose to take the environmental costs associated with datacentres directly, rather than being charged them for them indirectly via (say) occupancy costs. We haven't gone this far at JLP but we are now paying closer attention to tracking these costs.

Expert help

It is well worth commissioning a piece of consultancy work from a trusted, expert supplier to examine exactly how your datacentre is arranged, cooled, chilled and powered, and to recommend appropriate specific areas to improve that will save energy and emissions.

We commissioned such a study using an IBM expert in early 2008, and his findings, together with the work of our own staff and advice from BT too, indicated there was the potential for us to save 5–12% of the total energy bills by taking some simple remedial actions, recommendations we are now acting upon.

Some of the areas examined were:

- optimisation of the chilling and power facilities;
- our use of space for expansion and the implications for the total volume of air being circulated (maybe 10–20% more than required);
- cabinet positions and how these can best take advantage of datacentre 'hot-aisle/cold-aisle arrangements';
- minor floor leaks and misplaced vent tiles and the implications for cooling energy loss;
- flaws with the hot-aisle/cold-aisle arrangement itself (e.g. gaps allowing air to remix between the two).

This was then followed up by an advisory visit from two engineers from the company involved with the original design and installation of the equipment in our datacentre when it was first commissioned in 2002. Also present was a technical representative from our current server rack manufacturer.

We revalidated that the datacentre installation had been designed at the time to maximise 'free cooling' and to incorporate the most efficient air conditioning components then available (and still regarded as being amongst the best of breed today).

The consensus from all of these discussions was that the most benefit would accrue from our raising the temperature within the Computer Hall. We chose to do this initially from its then 21.5C to 23C, and to then follow this up in two single 1C steps until we were at 25C. We would allow a cautious two months after each step change to assess whether or not there were any issues, and agreed that the temperature could be reduced at any point should an issue arise.

As an aside, our experience of losing the air conditioning in a test and development server room on one occasion in summer 2006 was that the temperature rose extremely rapidly (see Figure 8). (Network infrastructure within our computer halls is generally well instrumented, and our datacentre core network switches currently have 43 different temperature sensors!) It could be argued that keeping computer halls slightly hotter will give us slightly less time to try to fix things in the event of a recurrence; however, we agreed that on balance it was worth proceeding with the change.

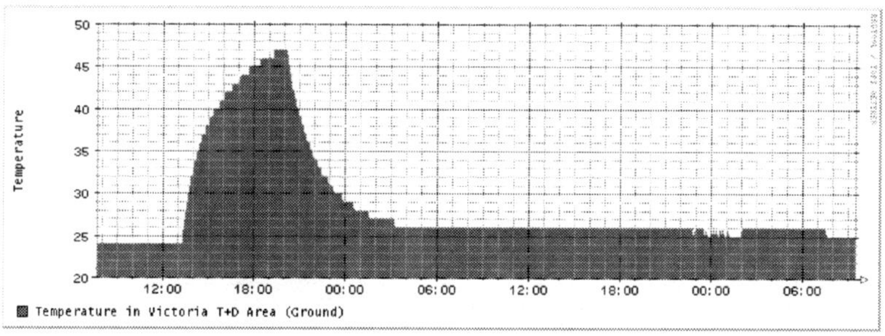

Figure 8: Rapid temperature rise

We have for the present discounted any changes to the humidity control in the room, but are aware that this is a possible area to revisit in the future. Humidity variations within a room controlled to a tight band of allowed humidity can lead to air conditioning units fighting to raise the humidity in one area and reduce it in another. Intel and others have widened the range of humidity allowed in their datacenters and seen cost savings.

There are a number of server benches of an open design installed within the server rack runs, as well as other gaps which we identified as adversely affecting the airflow. The solution we are adopting here is to modify the benches and fill the gaps with fitted blanking panels.

The racks that house most of our networking equipment have glass fronted doors, and this is true for the older server cabinets as well. Newer server cabinets have mesh doors which permit much greater airflow. This is an area we will keep under review as equipment densities and cooling requirements increase, and if we reduce the operational range of devices.

We are keen to validate the likely cost savings we might achieve from this overall project, but we do not have the sophistication in electricity cost apportioning across the campus where the datacentre is hosted. However, we are investigating options for upgrading the building management software to improve this granularity of reporting.

Beyond the steps mentioned above, other improvements are seen as either impractical, or of insignificant positive impact at this time. However, as technology changes, other options will undoubtedly present themselves to save more energy and reduce our carbon footprint further, and we will use the acorn diagram to track potential initiatives.

Where does the power go?

It's sobering to consider how much power is lost between its generation and its effective use in IT. Industry experts Steve O'Donnell (an ex-BTer who was responsible for successfully transforming the efficiency of their datacentres in recent years) and Steve Bowden (one of IBM's top green gurus) have taken me through calculations like the one below to show just how much potential there still is to up our game. The comments in italics give some pointers as to which industry trends might improve this ratio of power generated to effective power used.

- Traditional power stations are 30% efficient. So 70% is lost in (say) cooling towers.
    - *Combined heat and power (CHP) systems are very efficient by comparison.*
- Typically, 7% of that 30% is then lost in transmission across the national grid.
    - *Local generation is therefore more efficient.*
- Up to 50% of what makes it through to the datacentre is needed for cooling.
    - *Reduce the need for cooling through higher temperature operation. Challenge suppliers about perceived wisdom relating to temperature and humidity tolerance ratings.*
- At the datacentre we convert AC power to DC input to our lead-acid UPS batteries, then convert back to AC and then once again back to DC in the computer power supply. We see between 25% and 40% losses through these conversions

  - *Seriously consider taking DC power directly into the computer after the first conversion.*
- And then we use only 8% of the machine's capacity on average, **ending up with only about 1% of the energy with which we started actually doing useful work!**
  - *Virtualise and consolidate computing power as much as possible.*

CHAPTER 11: IT AS A GREEN ENABLER

This is the section of the book where we allow ourselves to briefly stop self-flagellating, worrying about IT's own carbon emissions, and turn our attention instead to some ideas for using IT to help reduce the other 98 percent (typically) of the organisation's carbon footprint. This is 'IT as saint rather than sinner', as I heard it expressed recently at the CIES conference[15] on Green IT in April 2008. Perhaps the carbon footprint of IT will even actually need to go up a little to make it all happen ('silicon offsetting' is a phrase we are starting to hear more and more to describe this). To get to grips with the 98% we need to think a lot more about systems development rather than just focusing as we have until now on infrastructure solutions.

Travel reduction and homeworking support

Much is written about the need to reduce travel and the opportunities for IT to remove the need for many employee journeys. And there are certainly some exciting technical developments which promise to help with this. Anyone who has used Cisco's Telepresence[16] facility to hold a meeting with someone at a remote location will have immediately been struck by how much of a step change the immersive experience is from that with previous generations of videoconferencing equipment. And virtual worlds offer an alternative means (albeit sometimes a rather too surreal an

---

[15] The CIES IT Conference, 'How Green is Your IT? Opportunity or Threat? Marketing Ploy or New Business Model?', 10–11 April 2008, Barcelona, Spain

[16] www.cisco.com/en/US/products/ps7060/index.html

alternative for many) to communicate with colleagues on the other side of the world.

Travelling between company sites is still necessary however, and indeed there are many occasions when it is absolutely right that a meeting takes place face to face rather than over a direct-to-desktop videophone, say. Perhaps the rule of thumb to remember here is *ensure that you actually derive value out of any travelling you actually do.*

Homeworking and flexible working

IT remote access solutions can certainly enable homeworking or flexible working for employees. Many of the communications technologies now becoming standard across enterprises, such as instant messaging, can improve the experience, too.

Homeworking is seen as green (especially if it can then result in fewer corporate offices and reduced heating and lighting requirements), but companies should double-check that in reducing their carbon footprints by making increased use of it they are not just shifting the problem to their employees' personal carbon footprints (in the winter a home that might not have needed heating will need to be warm, but this needs to be balanced against any reduced transport impact).

There are acceptance issues too, of course. One company I spoke to had received a flat refusal from staff concerned about having webcams installed on homeworking kit, as the employees felt they'd then need to tidy the house properly and not work in just their pyjamas!

Helping measure and report on the problem

If you have to calculate a carbon footprint then you're most likely using IT to do that. So business intelligence systems, company intranets and 'dashboard' displays all play their part in helping business tackle the problem. Software such as IBM's Carbon Analysis Tool[17] can help companies quantify the impact of various business activities and provide insights for 'carbon management'.

Where else might IT help?

Here are just a few examples of other areas IT could help address :

There is a significant monthly printing operation needed for payslips and pension slips, and there seems less and less reason not to make this an electronic record rather than require that printing. Indeed, routine printing of various reports is common to many IT systems. It is worth examining each major use of paper in turn and double-checking that the report in question is actually required.

Transport optimisation across an organisation's supply chain is a significant opportunity for IT to use scheduling software to help the business green itself and take unnecessary lorry trips off the roads.

Utility companies can use performance management systems, for example at a waste water treatment plant to greatly reduce the amount of energy used.

---

[17] www.ibm.com/news/ca/en/2008/05/2008_05_23.html

We can develop products using simulation systems rather than requiring that a physical product is built and tested, and this reduces waste.

I spoke recently with a member of the Meteorological Office IT department, who talked about the weather reporting systems they have in operation. The use of this data by the airline industry (route planning) and power stations (likely demand for energy) can make those industries' use of energy significantly more efficient.

SMART and a panda

The two best recent studies I have seen summarising the opportunities for IT are the Climate Group's study '*SMART 2020: Enabling the low carbon economy in the information age*' (www.smart2020.org) and the World Wildlife Fund's '*Outline for the first global IT strategy for CO_2 reductions*' (www.panda.org/ict).

SMART is an acronym explained in the Climate Group report as follows:

- **S**tandardise: provide information in standard forms on energy consumption and emissions, across sectors.
- **M**onitor: incorporate monitoring information into the design and control for energy use.
- **A**ccount: provide the capabilities and platforms to improve accountability of energy and carbon.
- **R**ethink: offer innovations that capture energy efficiency opportunities across buildings/homes, transport, power, manufacturing and other infrastructure and provide alternatives to current ways of operating, learning, living, working and travelling.

- **T**ransform: apply smart and integrated approaches to energy management of systems and processes, including benefits from both automation and behaviour change and develop alternatives to high carbon activities, across all sectors of the economy.

The World Wildlife Fund report identifies ten solutions (examples are smart buildings, smart appliances, and 'dematerialisation services' – essentially using 'bits instead of bricks'). The report discusses how each might be implemented, and crucially considers both positive ('low-carbon feedback') and negative ('high-carbon feedback') possible outcomes. It is ambitious in its scope, claiming that implementation of all ten areas could lead to an equivalent reduction of one billion tonnes of CO_2.

The task for IT departments such as ours now is to determine how we best engage with the rest of our organisations to apply those reports' findings to our businesses.

Green power generation

The SMART2020 study points out that an obvious way to reduce emissions is to use as much electricity as possible from renewable sources. Our companies can do this by 'purchasing renewable electricity, by installing renewable generation on their sites and by making renewable electricity integral to their products'. JLP has taken many such initiatives and for example began purchasing all of its energy as renewable in 2007. Our IT department's involvement in this area has so far been minimal, though. I would suggest that this will change in future. The sector as a whole is well placed to partner with power companies, help optimise the existing electricity grid to allow more efficient power distribution and enable the use of more renewable or green power.

There are solutions, and IT can take a lead

The potential solutions to the problem of reducing our carbon footprints are there in all of our organisations. They are not always obvious but we can find them. And the opportunity for IT is in thought leadership or as a role model for the rest of the organisation, not just in supplying systems or making infrastructure as efficient as possible.

APPENDIX 1: GREEN IT ACTION LIST

socitm insight

SOCITM (the Society of Information Technology Management) is an organisation which promotes the effective and efficient use of IT in local government and the public sector. A very good action list for Green IT, produced by a working group co-chaired by SOCITM, the Ministry of Defence and six local authorities, is available from the SOCITM website www.socitm.gov.uk. An adapted version of it is reproduced here with permission. Note that for reasons of space, the four right-hand columns (Status, Date started, Date embedded and Owner) have not been reproduced here.

Readers are advised to consult the SOCITM website to download the latest version of this document, as it is added to and updated regularly.

The SOCITM actions list provides a good starter for organisations to add to and develop their own Green IT action plans, and could be used to populate an initial 'acorns' or equivalent diagram and spreadsheet, with each action assessed against the attributes outlined in Chapter 3.

Appendix 1: Green IT action list

Equipment	Desired outcomes	Actions required	Comments
Office IT			
Desktops	Reduce desktop PC power consumption and associated cooling load	Put stickers on PCs: 'Not standby, OFF Please'"	
		Shut down PCs remotely after office hours if not logged on / holiday periods	
		Reduce volume of 'kit' per head	
		Enable active power management (standby/hibernate after a defined period of inactivity)	
Screens	Reduce monitor power consumption and associated cooling load	Replace old CRTs at end of life with LCD screens	
		Remove active screensavers	
		Switch monitors to standby automatically after 10 minutes of inactivity (no screensaver)	
TVs, AV equipment	Reduce power consumption and associated cooling load	Replace old CRTs at end of life with LCDs	
		Switch TVs and AV equipment off after use	

Printers, copiers	Reduce paper consumption	Install duplex printing as default setting in drivers on desktop PCs	
		At end of life, replace non-duplex with duplex printers	
		Culture: message 'Are you sure you want to print?'	
		Consider use of ID Cards and printing budgets	
		Auto default to greyscale/economy mode	
		Cartridges (refill options – and supplier to pick up used cartridges)	
		Install card- or code-based print job activation	
Printers, copiers, scanners, fax	Reduce power consumption	Replace individual printers, copiers, fax machines, scanners at end of life with shared multi-function devices	
		Print function turned off overnight	
		Metering of power consumption	
		Floor walker to power off equipment out of hours	
		FAX to email service	
		Enable power-saving sleep mode on printers	
		Put printers on timed power supply (automatically turn off power with manual override for out-of-hours use)	

Back-end IT (datacentre)

Servers, storage, telecoms equipment	Reduce power consumption (servers and cooling) through reduction in number of active servers	Identify machines that are running but not providing any services (shut down or reallocate to run active services). e.g. power down test/development environments out of hours	This depends on the development and implementation of an effective service catalogue (e.g.ITILv3). This issue can be exacerbated by the increasing use of virtualisation as a 'quick fix' in place of actually rationalising the software and service estate
		Optimise/consolidate servers	
		Consolidate services from many machines onto single-server (fewer servers needed)	
		Convert physical servers to 'virtual servers' – partition servers that run in parallel on the same hardware without any interference (e.g. VMware, Xen)	Does produce a benefit in terms of embedded energy, but less improvement in 'in use' energy, particularly if a SAN is deployed at the same time – with the additional overheads that brings
		Implement a strong set of business processes to control physical or virtual server sprawl, require strong justifications for any new device.	
		Implement an effective data management process to substantially reduce the total volume of data stored and therefore storage equipment	Do not waste money on vendor's hardware or software until you have a process that the storage management solution can support

		When provisioning new services, create 'virtual servers' instead of procuring physical new servers	Secondary risk here – virtualisation is not a cure for management issues; need to still question need for new servers
	Reduce power consumption through higher specifications and better configuration	Specify high-efficiency PSUs (80% conversion or better)	
		Specify low-power consumption CPUs	
		Turn off idle servers when not in use (mainly useful for batch processing)	Not always as easy as it sounds – consider impact on monitoring systems, and risk to PDUs
		Power down disks after defined period of inactivity	This is more applicable to disks in servers than SANs. Also, unlikely to have any impact on servers which are probed regularly by monitoring platforms and whose applications write checkpoints to logfiles regularly.
		Avoid mixed fragment metals	
	Reduce use of hazardous substances in manufacturing process or in products	Ensure equipment is compliant with relevant legislation (e.g. ROHS)	
	Maximise life-span of equipment	Ensure that equipment can be upgraded (e.g. disks, RAM)	Better perhaps to purchase only the hardware specification that is required within the next 24 months, if

			more capacity needed later, migrate the service then, and repurpose the old h/w.
	Maximise re-use of components and recycling of raw materials	Ensure that machine can be returned to manufacturer for disposal at end-of-life	Ask the manufacturer what proportion of the machine they are able to recover and reuse in their reprocessing facilities
		Audit trail after disposal/reuse	
		Ensure that supplier will arrange for re-use of equipment that is no longer required but is still serviceable	
		Ensure that equipment is designed to allow re-use of individual components	
		Ensure that use of non-recyclable components (e.g. PVC) is minimised	
Power supply	Minimise energy consumption in use	Ensure that equipment has a high efficiency power supply unit (PSU)	
		Ensure that equipment complies with Energy Star standards, and EPEAT regulations	
		Ensure that machine is supplied with power-saving features enabled and active	
Cooling	Reduce cooling power requirement through physical changes to cooling equipment and other plant	Use external air in winter as input to chillers (instead of re-circulating hot air)	
		Install variable speed fans and link speed of movement to actual heat conditions in the data centre (to reduce cooling in off-peak periods)	
		Install water cooling (instead of air cooling) systems	

		Switch off lights in datacentres or use natural light	
		Switch from AC to DC power distribution within data centre	There is currently some debate about whether this is appropriate…
		Install modular M&E equipment to reduce the energy loss of underutilisation	
		Run backup generators on bio-diesel	There is also some debate about whether this is appropriate…
	Reduce cooling power requirement through improved layout and configuration	Reduce cooling and increase the ambient room temperature; use curtains to promote airflow?	
		Reduce re-circulation of hot air over heat emitting equipment by creating physically separated cold-air/hot-air aisles for send/return of chilled air (passes through equipment from cold aisle to hot aisle)	
		Eliminate hot spots by repositioning equipment in the datacentre (thereby reduce overall temperature and overall cooling requirement)	

Through-life Green IT planning

Green disposals	Ensure CTOs are asking the right questions of suppliers	Ensure vendor buyback disposal programme provides an accredited audit trail whether for re-use, resale or recycle	
		The audit trail should provide a parts-based disposal schedule if item is being sent to recycle	
		Compliance with local and regional statutory requirements, such as the RoHS	

		Supply chain ISO14000 series certification should be recommended to all suppliers	
		Value assessment of asset prior to vendor collection VfM ROI assurance scheme	
		Consider 3rd sector or charitable donation	
		Warning! If equipment is damaged, e.g. monitors, then it is classified as hazardous waste and must meet Environment Agency certification both for transport and disposal. Registration is required.	
		PC erasure must include all software licences from the hard drive. Ensure your supplier has done so.	
		If the equipment is in working order it can be collected by your supplier, but if it is damaged in any way an official audit trail, down to the site accepting the equipment for landfill, must be registered and tracked	
		Ensure that your contractors remove cartridges from printers prior to reuse, resale or recycle, and that they send items to your recycling agent.	
		Ask your suppliers the question: what is your landfill avoidance breakdown?	Land avoidance benchmark: MoD, DE&S, Disposal Services Authority, landfill avoidance currently 97%
		WEEE directive compliance: Many Government contracts are let through third parties, intermediaries, outsourcing contracts etc., that are not always mandated to comply with WEEE. Please ensure in writing that any provision through your department explicitly binds your intermediary to comply with WEEE.	

Telecommunications

Mobile phones	Reduction in the number of devices	Consolidate multiple handsets (phone, PDA, etc.) into a single multi-function unit (at end-of-life points)	
	Refresh	Review refresh cycle on mobile phones	
	Refresh	Challenge purchase decisions to reflect longer life of device	
	Reduction in the use of scarce resources, reduction in cost	When changing service providers keep handset and change SIM only	
	Reduction in energy bills	When purchasing new phone request chargers that use no power when not in use	
	Reduction in energy bills	When purchasing new phone request chargers that turn themselves off when the charge is complete	Exert pressure on suppliers to introduce batteries that auto switch off
	Reduction in the amount of times needed to have handset charged	Request long-life, energy-efficient batteries	
	Optimisation of handset usage	When purchasing new phones use battery life as a priority purchasing scoring	
	Reduction in land fill and toxic land fill avoidance, reuse of scarce resources	When disposing of mobile phones, ensure that charitable donations are taken into consideration	
Desktop Phones	Reduction in energy bills	When purchasing new desktop phones use energy usage as a priority scoring criteria	
	Reduction in energy bills	Consider VoIP when replacing desktop phone	

	Reduction in cost, right-sizing equipment, reduction in energy bills, reduction in training requirements	Consider a multi-tier desktop phone policy (everyone does not need the greatest executive version of the desktop phone)	
	Travel substitution	Consider desktop integrated video conferencing equipment when replacing desktop phones	
	Reduction in land fill and toxic land fill avoidance, reuse of scarce resources	Ensure that machine can be returned to manufacturer for disposal at end-of-life	
	Reduction in land fill and toxic land fill avoidance, reuse of scarce resources	Ensure that supplier will arrange for re-use of equipment that is no longer required but is still serviceable	
	Reduction in land fill and toxic land fill avoidance, reuse of scarce resources	Ensure that equipment is designed to allow re-use of individual components	
	Reduction in use of scarce resources, cost savings	Ensure that new equipment has reusable plug components so that devices can use previous charging systems	
	Regulatory requirement	Ensure that all equipment is PAT tested prior to re-use or resale (charitable donations)	
	Reduction in toxic land fill	Ensure that use of non-recyclable components (e.g. PVC) is minimised	
Power supply	Reduction in energy bills	Ensure that equipment has a high-efficiency power supply unit (PSU)	
	Reduction in energy bills	Ensure that equipment complies with Energy Star standards	
	Reduction in energy bills	Ensure that machine is supplied with power-saving features enabled and active	

APPENDIX 2: FURTHER RESOURCES

APC White papers	www.apc.com
'Badbuster'	www.badbuster.com
Business Green	www.businessgreen.com
The Carbon Trust	www.carbontrust.co.uk
Corporate IT Forum ('tif.')	www.tif.co.uk
DEFRA Market Transformation Programme	www.mtprog.com
Department for Business Enterprise and Regulatory Reform (WEEE directive)	www.berr.gov.uk
'The Ecobutton'	www.eco-button.com
Energy – Beyond Oil, Armstrong F and Blundell K, Oxford University Press (2007)	ISBN 0-199209-96-0
Energy Star standards	www.energystar.gov
EPEAT	www.epeat.net
'The Ethics of Climate Change – Pay Now or Pay More Later?' (*Scientific American*)	www.sciam.com/earth-and-environment
Gartner	www.gartner.com
Global Action Plan UK	www.globalactionplan.org.uk (includes a link to *An Inefficient*

	Truth full report)
The Green Data Center: Steps for the Journey (draft)	available from www.ibm.com/redbooks
The Green Grid	www.thegreengrid.org
'Greenpeace Guide to Consumer Electronics'	www.greenpeace.org/electronics
An Inconvenient Truth	www.climatecrisis.net
John Lewis Partnership	www.johnlewispartnership.co.uk
Northwest Product Stewardship Council (US)	www.productstewardship.net
ROHS directive	www.rohs.gov.uk
The Rough Guide to Climate Change, Henson R, Rough Guides Ltd (2006)	ISBN 1-843537-11-7
SMART 2020: Enabling the low carbon economy in the information age	www.smart2020.org
Society of Information Technology Management (in the public sector)	www.socitm.gov.uk
VeryPC – Principles in Computing	www.very-pc.co.uk
WWF Outline for the first global IT strategy for CO_2 reductions	www.panda.org/ict

ITG RESOURCES

IT Governance Ltd source, create and deliver products and services to meet the real-world, evolving IT governance needs of today's organisations, directors, managers and practitioners. The ITG website www.itgovernance.co.uk is the international one-stop shop for corporate and IT governance information, advice, guidance, books, tools, training and consultancy.

At www.itgovernance.co.uk/green-it.aspx you will find a comprehensive range of books, tools and standards for Green IT and environmental management systems. Green IT training is also available through this site.

www.itgovernanceusa.com provides a complete range of IT governance books and tools into North America from our US logistics base.

Pocket Guides

For full details of the entire range of Pocket Guides listed below, simply follow the links at www.itgovernance.co.uk/publishing.aspx.

Practical Information Security Pocket Guides

- A Dictionary of Information Security Terms, Abbreviations and Acronyms
- ISO27001: Assessments without Tears
- ISO27001: A Pocket Guide
- Risk Assessment for Asset Owners
- Practical IT Governance Pocket Guides
- IT Governance
- IT Regulatory Compliance in the UK
- IT Regulatory Compliance in North America

Toolkits

ITG's unique range of toolkits includes the IT Governance Framework Toolkit, which contains all the tools and guidance that you will need in order to develop and implement an appropriate IT governance framework for your organisation. Full details can be found at www.itgovernance.co.uk/ products/519.

For a free paper on how to use the proprietary CALDER-MOIR IT Governance Framework, and for a free trial version of the toolkit, see www.itgovernance.co.uk/calder_moir.aspx.

Best Practice Reports

ITG's new range of Best Practice Reports is now at: www.itgovernance.co.uk/best-practice-reports.aspx. These offer you essential, pertinent, expertly researched information on an increasing number of key issues.

Training and Consultancy

IT Governance also offers training and consultancy services across the entire spectrum of disciplines in the information governance arena. Details of training courses can be accessed at www.itgovernance.co.uk/training.aspx and descriptions of our consultancy services can be found at http://www.itgovernance.co.uk/consulting.aspx.

Why not contact us to see how we could help you and your organisation?

Newsletter

IT governance is one of the hottest topics in business today, not least because it is also the fastest moving, so what better way to keep up than by subscribing to *Sentinel*, ITG's free monthly newsletter? It provides monthly updates and resources across the whole spectrum of IT governance subject matter, including risk management, information security, ITIL and IT service management, project governance, compliance and so much more. Subscribe for your free copy at: www.itgovernance.co.uk/newsletter.aspx.

Printed in the United Kingdom by
Lightning Source UK Ltd., Milton Keynes
142057UK00001B/15/P

9 781905 356614